CW00345926

ORPINGTON 127

THE AUTOBIOGRAPHY OF A WAR BABY

BY

MICHAEL PROOM

**Grosvenor House
Publishing Limited**

All rights reserved
Copyright © Michael Proom, 2013

The right of Michael Proom to be identified as the author of this
work has been asserted by him in accordance with Section 78
of the Copyright, Designs and Patents Act 1988

The book cover picture is copyright to Michael Proom

This book is published by
Grosvenor House Publishing Ltd
28-30 High Street, Guildford, Surrey, GU1 3EL.
www.grosvenorhousepublishing.co.uk

This book is sold subject to the conditions that it shall not, by way of
trade or otherwise, be lent, resold, hired out or otherwise circulated
without the author's or publisher's prior consent in any form of binding or
cover other than that in which it is published and
without a similar condition including this condition being imposed
on the subsequent purchaser.

A CIP record for this book
is available from the British Library

ISBN 978-1-78148-637-5

For Sarah and Andrew

ACKNOWLEDGEMENTS

To all of my friends mentioned in this book who have contributed their own memories of our youthful years: to Graham, Harry, Howard and Colin (amongst others.)

With a special acknowledgement to my good friend John Baker whose almost photographic memory of our time at Grammar School together in the 1950s provided many an anecdote for this book.

"Past Purple": a history of Chislehurst and Sidcup Grammar School by Charles Wells and John Hazelgrove

BBC History website
historyorb.com
Wikipaedia.com
Encyclopaedia Britannica

Nigel Walker, Headmaster, Chislehurst and Sidcup Grammar School for his kind help and interest in this book of remembrances.

Steve Crampton. Present owner of my childhood home for his hospitality.

PROLOGUE

I was born on 11th April 1943. The following day the final elements of Rommel's Afrika Corps surrendered to the British 8th Army under General Montgomery in Northern Tunisia. The World would remain at war for another two years.

I should have been born down the road in Orpington Hospital but as that had been requisitioned as a Military Hospital for the Canadians my Mother had been taken a few miles away to the Cottage Hospital at St Paul's Cray. My earliest memory of life is lying in my pram on the verandah of our house and seeing the sky turn dark with indistinct shapes. Much later I learned that these had in fact been Bomber aircraft assembling over the the nearby RAF base at Biggin Hill to meet with their fighter escorts before leaving to bomb Germany.

My father's name was Harry, my Mother's Hilda May. Not that this really mattered very much! Dad always called Mum Molly and she always called him Bill. I never did find out why this was the case. Such intimacies just are. Dad was one of the country's leading Micro-Bacteriologists. He had a Doctorate from Kings College London. He was a short stocky man with a moustache and a fun loving personality. Mum was maybe an inch or two taller, with dark hair and was an attractive lady.

Dad came from a family of academics. As I remember them growing up, they were a rather stuffy bunch, brought up in the

Edwardian era with associated social values and mores. His Father had been Headmaster of a Grammar School, as was his brother my Uncle Tom. His sister – my Aunt Dorothy – was Headmistress of a Primary School in Kempston in Bedfordshire. His other sister – Aunt Kitty – was a UK Ladies Chess Champion. Married to Alec Terrett, an Income Tax Inspector. Aunt Dorothy was quite fun in a dry sort of a way.

Mum came from humbler stock. Her Father had been a Tea taster – an important part of the huge Tea Trade with India. I am afraid that whereas Dad loved her dearly, I always felt that some of his siblings considered Mum to be a bit *infra dig*. Both my Grandfathers had died before I was born. Nanny Tanner – my maternal Grandmother – lived with us. She was a dear old soul, South London salt of the Earth to the core. I can never remember her out of her pinafore around the house.

My paternal Grandmother on the other hand lived in a Nursing Home down the road in Chislehurst. She was an imperious and God fearing woman who most strongly believed that the Sabbath should be respected - no-one should work on Sundays. This maxim however did not extend apparently to those who brought her her breakfast or made her bed.

Due to his particular scientific speciality being a reserved occupation, and as a part of the team that advised the War Office on chemical and bacteriological weapons, Dad did not actually go into combat. When at home he did his stint as APR Warden with the rest of the local men. Our house was on what the local Estate Agents still call today "the exclusive Knoll Estate", at 6 Stanley Road. We had a fairly spacious 3 bed semi detached house, with a long wide back garden with privet hedges bounding the house on one side, with no fewer than 11 fruiting apple trees – Cookers and Cox's Orange. There was a bullace tree, a type of small damson, on the other side, and at the bottom of the garden there was a rather tumbledown greenhouse with a large fertile vine producing succulent bunches of reddish mauve grapes every summer.

"Dig for victory" was the national creed during WW2. Every square foot of bare earth in Britain, from flower beds to 10 acre fields, was turned over to the growing of vegetables or wheat. At home we ourselves had always had fresh apples for part of the year; we wrapped the remainder in newspaper and kept them in the dark depths of the coal cellar for the winter. We grew our own fresh vegetables and tomatoes and even had grapes to eat in the summer.

In the front garden there were three Russet apple trees, a huge Orange Blossom shrub, a large Chinese lantern bush and a laurel tree. Along the frontages of our house and Number 4 a trailing lime tree hedge had been grown above the fence. On the left two thirds of the way down the back garden was the Air Raid shelter – not just any old Nissen hut for us, but a good solid concrete shelter, the walls sunk into the earth and three steps down turn right to the blast proof area. I can to this day still smell the dank mustiness of that shelter.

I am the first to give thanks that I had not been born in one of the many towns or cities in Britain that had been bombed flat in the Blitz. Orpington as a whole had remained essentially immune from the ravages of more than 5 years of war. In our house in Stanley Road my parents and I lived a peaceful, quiet existence, as did the residents in the other streets on the Knoll Estate - in Lucerne Road, Keswick Road, St Kilda Road – named after places which I assume that when the houses had been built in the '30s the Developer had obviously selected to be refined enough. (Maybe Stanley had been a relative?) The Knoll even had its own Country Club at the end of Lucerne on Knoll Rise. It was a solid, respectable - and especially a safe - middle class enclave

This semi pastoral peace and quiet was severely shaken on the morning of 27th March 1945, when the last German V2 rocket to hit Britain fell on Kynaston Road, 50 yards behind Carlton Parade, the parade of shops right at the end of the High Street at the junction with Court Road. Less than a mile as the crow flew from our home. It is reckoned that had it not been for the rear wall of the Carlton cinema taking the brunt of the blast there would have been many more deaths. If it had struck when the cinema was full of film goers — but mercifully it hadn't. Amazingly only one person, an unlucky housewife, was killed.

The Germans had developed two types of *Vergeltungswaffen* (V weapons) during 1944. The first of these "Revenge Weapons" had been the V1, fondly known to all in the UK as the "Doodlebug". This was a type of crude pilot-less aircraft capable of around 300mph. First fired in June of that year, as it approached you could hear the dull drone of its rocket motor. If the sound stopped overhead, you ducked as this meant it was coming to Earth. Thousands of these were fired at Southern Britain, and after D Day at military targets such as Antwerp.

They were subsonic, so many of them were shot down by anti-aircraft fire Many more were brought down by RAF Spitfires. They shot them down, and also developed the technique of flying alongside them and positioning their wing under the fin of the V1 and then flipping them over into empty fields.

The V2 on the other hand was a much more sinister weapon, and had represented a real threat to Britain. Supersonic, firing a war head 50 miles into a sub space trajectory, it was the first true Inter Continental Ballistic Missile. There was no defence against it. Too high and too fast to track on radar or shoot down, it went at several times the speed of sound, creating the eerie effect that you only heard it arriving after it had already detonated on the ground. The first V2 was fired in September

1944. If D Day had been 6 months later, the defeat of Germany might have taken longer.

But why had Orpington suddenly become a strategic target for Berlin? Well according to stories that I have heard since, Military Intelligence in Whitehall had managed to convince the Germans that their V2 strikes had been overshooting London by 10 – 15 miles. As a result the German Rocketeers had been resetting their gyroscopes - which explains why the last salvoes of firings had all landed in Kent Our own Government had been trying to get us killed!.

Now of course apart from the vague imprint on the memory of dark shapes in the sky I can remember absolutely nothing of the above events. I had just reached the age of 2 when the war ended. I should also add that trying to recover childhood memories going back over 60 years has not been the easiest of tasks. Therefore, whereas I am pretty sure that the events and personal experiences that I describe in the book are factual, it has proved simply impossible to always get them in the correct chronological order.

That is why, in the first few chapters particularly, I jump backwards and forwards in time as a particular subject crops up. This is so as both to expand on the subject and to emphasize the importance of it in respect of its overall effect on my psyche. And more importantly on the differences in the Society of the post war years to that of the Society that we live in today. For despite all the hardships and austerity I believe that the immediate post war years were for many of us children a golden age for childhood the like of which we shall never see again.

CHAPTER 1

My Mother died in December 2010 at the age of 97. They were tough old birds the Mothers of the War years. My wife's Mother died at 104, my Best Man's Mother made it to 95, and his wife's Mother is still going strong at 92 – after having served in the SOE in German occupied France. Many people put forward two main reasons for the longevity of women of my Mother's generation. The first and most obvious one being that they did not go to war. Hundreds of thousands of their menfolk died in battle in WW2. Over 25,000 more perished in Japanese Prisoner of War camps.

The other reason women of that generation enjoyed longevity was THEY had had no stress in their daily lives. They had kept house and raised their families. Every other single decision and duty had been left to the man of the house. Married women simply did NOT go out to work.

World War 11 began to put the final nail in that chauvinist coffin. Apart from the hundreds of thousands of women who worked in the Ammunition factories and other essential manufacturing, and the hundreds of thousands of land girls who dug for victory, there were of course the hundreds of thousands of war widows - and millions of ordinary housewives - who had had to use every scrap of their ingenuity to feed and clothe their families on what had been little more than starvation rations.

Have you ever snacked on Pignut – *conopodium majus*? A member of the parsley family, its roots are nutritious and taste nutty. We children in the war years often did, as we were usually hungry. There were no crisps, no chocolate bars, no packet snacks of any description at all. The best you might find were sherbet dips and striped humbugs dating from pre war for special occasions. It may well come as a huge shock to anyone born after 1960 to learn that from 1941 until as late as 1954 food, clothing, petrol and furniture had all been strictly rationed in Britain. The following are the ACTUAL weekly rationed amount of each major foodstuff per person laid down by the Ministry of Food in 1941. You were given a Ration Book and the grocer had to stamp the allowances.

Bacon and Ham	57 gms IN TOTAL per fortnight
Cheese	43 gms per week.
Butter / Margarine	50 gms / 198 gms per week
Cooking Fats	57 gms per week
Meat	1 shilling's worth (5p's worth!) per week
Sugar	227 gms per week
Tea	57 gms per week
Eggs	(not rationed per se but 1 per Ration Book when available)
Milk	3 pints per week.

The balance of the national diet came from vegetables, especially potatoes, bread: and from Fish, which was not rationed. Fish were abundant in our coastal waters. Fish represented the major source of protein in our wartime diet; maybe the only meaningful source. As any dietitian will tell you, Protein builds muscle and aids body growth. Which explains why – genetic disposition excepted – many men of my generation have sons a head and shoulders taller.

There would have been even more fish if the main North Sea fishing grounds round Iceland had not been closed to our fleets due to the German U Boat activity. It was this U Boat activity that had forced rationing upon Britain. In peacetime we had been importing 20 million tons of foodstuffs per annum. 50% of our meat, 70% of our cheese and sugar, over 75% of our cereals and fruit had come from overseas. The German U Boat campaign had been specifically designed to cut those supply lines. To starve us into surrender.

(After horrendous shipping losses in the first months of the War, Allied shipping carrying food, fuel and vital raw materials to Britain from North America and from the Empire was formed into convoys of maybe 60 – 75 Merchant vessels escorted by Warships. It was a campaign that went down to the wire. Over 3,000 Merchant ships and 150 warships on our side were sunk. Over 750 German submarines. The Battle of the Atlantic was a very close run thing.)

In addition to rations, every child had to have a large spoonful of a sticky malt extract called VIROL each week to ensure they had the desired amount of vitamins. Anyone who had to take VIROL will never forget the taste. Not unpleasant, but quite unique. Aside from the sick or those with special dietary needs these ration limits were rigorously applied.

With one exception - the Olympic Games that were held in London in 1948. Known forever after as the Austerity Games, British competitors were allowed DOUBLE rations. Compare that with the high protein / carbohydrate diets, special food supplements and isotonic drinks used by every athlete today. In 1948 the British competitors had even been obliged to make their own sports kit!. There were no sponsors, no commercial ties. All they had was spirit and courage to drive them on. They were the true unadulterated Olympians.

If anything rationing had become more severe after the war had ended. It even affected childrens' Education. In 1947 / 48 there was a national paper shortage. Schools combated this by asking children to use very small writing. Ink was of the poorest quality, so the end result was often impossible to read. Meat especially continued to be strictly rationed – even in 1951, six years after the war had ended you could still only buy 10 pennies worth (4p) of meat per week. Meat rationing lasted until 1954. According to the laws of Economics this drove the price of fish to almost stratospheric levels.

But Mum had not just had to juggle food rations to feed us. Many other household items were also rationed. A 340gm packet of soap powder had to last 2 weeks. A Central Office of Information film made in 1943 showed a picture of a bar of soap left in a pool of dishwater to dissolve.

The jingle ran

"Somebody's going to be sorry
"Somebody's going to pay
"Somebody's going to be sorry
"They wasted my life away"

Clothes were also rationed, with points awarded to individual items that also could only be bought with Ration books being stamped. Like millions of wives, Mum had to become a seamstress and take up knitting to clothe the family from old clothes. In the shops utility clothing that used a minimum of cloth were also introduced. No scrap of material was ever thrown away. Petrol was also strictly rationed until 1950 – so people no longer bought cars. Furniture was only available to newly weds or to those who had been bombed out of their homes.

Rationing ended finally in 1954 – when I was 11 years old. By that time there had been shortages of everything for almost 14 years. That fact had left a profound and indelible impression on the psyches of most Wartime Wives and Mothers that would stay with them for the rest of their days. It certainly affected Mum for the rest of her life.

What we today would consider meanness was for her probably simply precautionary - in case the Hun ever came back Over the subsequent years she had always given me, my brother Phil and her grand kids what can only be described as jumble sale knick knacks for our respective birthdays and Christmases. Either a plastic toy car with a 60p price tag on the bottom for our son, or for Phil a tartan "tam- o - shanter" that looked like it had once belonged to Harry Lauder. Second hand clothes two sizes too big went to my wife and daughter. She also seemed to have an endless supply of shop soiled green £1 notes - which she continued to hand out to family members long after they had ceased to become legal tender in the mid 70s.

I am afraid that I took her to task rather strongly several times for this, and for all the other cheap charity shop presents she had been giving the kids over the years. They felt she just did not have any affection for them. The rift lasted several years. I realise now that I may have been a tad hasty – perhaps after her war experiences she had seen these as worthwhile items to be saved and only given away for special occasions.?

(When Mother remarried in 1977 – after 14 years as a widow - and sold 6 Stanley we found hidden at the back of the larder tins of ham and fruit going back to the war years, as well as a cache of Kilner jars filled with Mum's home made gooseberry jam from fruit we had grown in the garden. This had been one of her great culinary triumphs in an age of austerity. We ate the jam gleefully, and the tinned peaches. Sadly the ham was beyond redemption.)

Talking with friends today they all report the same traits in their own Mothers – over careful with money, throwing nothing away, re-using materials and so forth. The result of scrimping and hoarding and making ends meet in the war years - whilst always wondering when the bomb with their family's name on it might arrive. 14 years of that left an indelible scar on the psyche. Sorry Ma.

Despite the depths of austerity in which we lived, most of the infant and childhood deaths of that era came from diptheria, measles, smallpox, tuberculosis - and of course there was the scourge of polio. If you had been lucky enough to dodge those, then the aforementioned "starvation rations" had kept you alive. My brother Phil and I were fortunate to have never contracted anything worse than the measles. I also clearly remember our Doctor, Peter Scales, who lived at the bottom of Scads Hill. He would always come out to tend to any chest conditions or fevers we might contract at any time of the day - or in the middle of the night.

He worked alone with no partners in the early days of the National Health Service. Doctors of the era earned £ 2,000 a year. Maybe £40,000 + in today's money. For this he was on call 24/7. How different this was to the pampered GPs of today. Usually in a partnership of several others, and despite the fact they earn up to £100K p.a, none of them is ever prepared to make house calls out of hours on a rota basis. They work a 5 day week, leaving any serious cases arising during the weekend to emergency Locums who never know your name and have little or no access to your medical records.

Hippocrates be damned – never on a Sunday...

Anyhow, what did not feature on the list of childhood ailments in the austerity years was Obesity. Not surprising, when a Double Bacon and Cheese Burger and chips today would have expended a fair proportion of the Wartime WEEKLY food allowance. Also sugar was severely rationed, so there was no confectionery produced in Britain from 1941 to 1948. So when

I hear the the word austerity being bandied around here there and everywhere in 2012 I have to give a wry smile. People of today's consumerist society (of which I have always been an active and enthusiastic member) under the age of 50 have no real conception of what the word really entails.

Yes the present recession has made life hard for many people in the last few years. Just imagine then how hard it would be to live through A WHOLE DECADE of strict rationing of food, clothing, furniture, petrol, with little or nothing in the shops to buy even if you had the money.: an enforced NON - consumer society. This was Britain in the years 1941 – 1951.

CHAPTER 2

For the first years of my life the Knoll Estate generally and Stanley Road in particular were the centre of my world. Our house was typical of the area and time. Built sometime in the 1930s, it had a red tiled doorstep that Mum always kept well polished. Inside the front door was a well lit hallway with coloured patterns in the window glass. Down the Hall the first on the right was the Front Room – kept for best it had a huge gilt framed mirror on one wall. I would spend a lot of time in this room in my teens, using it first as a music room and then later as somewhere to take girls. The next door off the Hall led to the Dining room and Lounge area. Wooden French windows led on to a verandah. This would become the TV room - eventually.

Both living rooms had open fire grates. Domestic Central Heating did not exist in the 40s or 50s. All houses were bitterly cold in winter. Mother used to wear a coat and hat to do housework upstairs on really cold days. The kitchen was perhaps the warmest place thanks to the coke fired Hot Water boiler. We huddled round the coal fire in the Dining Room in the evenings. It was a brave man who went into the Front room on a cold day when there was no fire. It was an ice box. It was just as well then that at that time most of the clothes we wore were woollen. Vests socks shirts trousers were all woollens.

The females in the family circle – Mothers, sisters, Aunts – would all be endlessly knitting scarves, sweaters, gloves. The big advantage of wool over man made fibres is that it can be endlessly darned when it becomes worn. (*And fed on grass!*) Mother would sit in front of the fire in the evening with a big darning mushroom in her hand over which would be stretched a sock with a hole in it to be mended. You would grow out of things before they finally fell apart. Men's socks lasted for years. Nowadays, as it is impossible to darn polyester or cotton or other man made materials we just throw old clothes away or give them to charity. Cheaper to go to Primark for new ones than to spend an hour darning them or a week knitting them. This is called the Consumer Society.

Only if you have been brought up in a house with coal or log fires can you know the unique feeling of all pervading warmth, well being, comfort and reflection it instils in to your psyche to gaze into the flickering flames of an open fire (behind the fire guard now!) on a cold winter's night. Overall you will be warmer with modern Central Heating – but as an emotional experience - well there is none. Coal fires had another major health benefit – they created updraughts in the chimney flue that sucked in fresh air, changing the air in the room constantly. I am convinced that this was the main reason why childhood asthma was almost unheard of in the 50s. With modern Central Heating and double glazing, the air just gets recirculated and less healthy as the day goes on. Aerosol use just makes it worse.

Coal fires had a built in disadvantage of course. You had to store the fuel somewhere, and lug it into the house. You had to clear out the ashes from the grate every morning, fire black the surrounds every so often. Well worth the trouble. Better than hypothermia.

The kitchen was off to the left past the stairs. It had a rather unusual design feature. The left hand side had a table and chairs, on the right was the coke fired boiler set into a rather large wall to ceiling tiled alcove, over which hung two large weighty contraptions on pulleys for hanging clothes to dry. In this unusually large alcove were the wash boiler - and the mangle. It is very possible that nobody born after 1960 will have any idea what this latter monstrosity was. A heavy metal frame set with twin rollers with a large winding handle through which Mum ran clothes fresh from the boiler to literally press the water out of them into a large bucket type contraption before hanging them up to dry.

In the corner on the right was the pantry, and next to that the cooker – which burned Gas. Not the clean odourless Natural Gas from the North Sea we use today, but Town Gas, a by - product of the carbonisation process that turned coal into coke. The resulting Gas was piped away and stored in huge circular Gasometers. These were to be found in every town in Britain. The Gasometers rose and fell in their metal frames according to the amount of the gas being stored.

It was perhaps one of the most ecologically unfriendly fuel production methods ever devised by man. It would cost untold millions to clear and decontaminate the sites when Town Gas was phased out in the 60s and 70s. Some were deemed TOO expensive to remove and can still be seen to this day. The most famous perhaps being the one overlooking the Oval Cricket Ground.

One of the by- products of Town Gas production however - the foul smelling smoke filled with tar condensate particles – was supposedly a recommended cure for chest conditions. Many a parent would take a child suffering from bronchitis, a common childhood complaint in those days, down to the gasworks to sniff the air. The results were beneficial. I can vouch for that personally.

Our whole house was heated by coal. Every house was. If there was one thing Britain had an abundance of in the 40s and 50s it was coal. Britain had literally thousands of coal mines in those days. Coal fuelled domestic homes, Business premises, Railways, Factories and the Power stations that provided the electricity. The country was almost totally energy independent. The Oil Industry in the Middle East and Persia (now Iran) was dominated by British Petroleum and Shell, so we also had unlimited access to oil. Petrol was still rationed then though.

The whole of the outside kitchen wall was taken up by a large coal bunker. The side of the house, in front of the back of the garage, was disappointing – a bare concrete area that had started to crack, sloping gently to a drain to run off the rain. Maybe the developer had run out of cash? There was another bunker down the side of the garage that held coke.

My parents had the front bedroom, and mine was at the back overlooking the lawn and vegetable garden with views over Orpington into the middle distance. I had my own coal fire! On a clear night I could hear the trains a mile or so away.

In November 1947 my brother Philip was born. He was named after the new husband of Princess Elizabeth. Once out of his cot Phil took the front bedroom overlooking the driveway. Dear old Nanny Tanner had to be evicted., and went to live with relatives in Erith.

Two months before Phil's arrival I had started full time Education at the age of 4 years and five months. I was reminded of this when my brother and I cleared out Mum's papers after her death. Amongst them I found my first school report – for the Autumn term of 1947 – for St Nicholas Preparatory School, Mayfield Avenue Orpington. (Long gone sadly) From this I can see that the veritable Miss Harwood had given me an A for French. My talent for languages was already beginning to show through even that early on.

St Nicholas was a small private Prep school. I have a vague recollection of Miss Harwood, a matronly figure in a pinafore, and of sloping lawns - and not a great deal else The school lay perhaps ½ mile from our house. What I do remember – which may well shock parents today – is that in my second year I used to walk there on my own most days. Up Stanley Rd I would go, in my little green blazer and cap, then left down one of the alleyways that still criss cross the Knoll Estate to Lucerne Road, up to the T junction, turn right down Knoll Rise and there you were.

Now I would no more think of letting a small person do this today than fly in the air. But it was 1948 and it had been safe for two reasons. First, there were fewer than 2.5 million registered motor vehicles of all types in the country – and due to petrol rationing most of these were not on the road at any one time. The cars that were could manage perhaps 65mph at most, and took an eternity to reach it – a following wind and a steep downward incline were also always handy. So there was no threat from boy racers. Or from the bald headed beer bellied bully boys in their oversized Japanese SUVs who prowl our roads today (Japan at the time had been an irradiated and defeated nation occupied by the American Army) White van man would not start to appear for another 25 years at least.

The other main reason had been the fact that – to me at least from the point of view of a 5 year old - there certainly seemed to be a warmth and overriding geniality and good nature, friendliness and public spiritedness within all sectors of society. Whether it was a Mother going to the shops or taking their own offspring to school, or a deliveryman, or a workman or a road sweeper, everyone would smile and say hello. And I was not the only little boy who walked to St Nicholas on his own. My chum Colin lived down the far end of Lynwood Drive from St Nicholas. He was in my year. Talking to him recently - after tracking down both him and a bunch of other old friends that feature later in this book – he told me that he too used to walk to school unattended. He too finds it amazing he could do so in complete safety.

I guess that being small boys had helped. But there certainly seemed to have been a common esprit de corps and a sense of national unity. I guess that in 1947, the whole populace had been exhausted by the war years and aggression in society seemed to be absent. To have survived the carnage had instilled everybody with relief enough. Adversity was now breeding social cohesion. In the immediate post war years Britain had been a very safe place in which to grow up.

This is more than borne out by the official Government Crime statistics for the period*. These show that in 1940 indictable offences stood at just 10 per 1,000 head of population. They then shrank back to just 8 in 1,000 in 1950, before rising back to 10 in 1960, 38 in 1970 and 40 in 1980. So in the first 17 years of my life crime levels had remained consistently at the lowest levels ever recorded. Theft and robbery had had no purpose – no-one had had much worth stealing. This went for car theft as well. Petrol was rationed, so cars were largely irrelevant.

So if you needed to get anywhere in the 6 years after the war had ended, before petrol rationing ended in 1950, you had just two choices - Public Transport or Shank's pony. British Rail connected Orpington to the outside world. It is just under 25 miles from Orpington Station to the Central London Rail Termini of Charing Cross and Victoria. Dad only had to go as far as Beckenham, several stations down the line, to reach the Wellcome Research Labs at Park Langley. Southern Region operated one of the most extensive commuter rail networks in the world. Still does of course. Under a new banner. The service

*(House of Commons Research paper 1999/111)

was essential for travel to work in the Capital. The lines had been electrified in the 30s. Every morning around 0700hrs lines of men in three piece suits, many wearing bowler hats and carrying furled umbrellas, would converge on Orpington Station on foot from all points of the compass.

Up until the Beeching report of 1963 that would decimate the rail network, closing some 2,000 stations and 5,000 miles of track, nearly all Freight and Manufactured Goods had been transported by Rail from factory, plant, quarry or coal mine and delivered to the railway station nearest to the customer. From there they were either delivered by van – or horse and cart – to the end user. Or collected by the customer themselves. Road haulage over longer distances was fairly limited at that time Fuel had been rationed until 1950.

As a further example of how vital the train was in those days to social mobility, I remember when we used to visit quite regularly one of my parents' friends in Wallington in Surrey (30 mins + by car today). We would walk nearly a mile to Orpington Station, and then catch a train to Penge East. We then alighted and walked over half a mile to Penge West station, where we would take another train to Wallington. We then walked for what seemed like another mile at least until we reached our destination. With me trotting along beside Phil in his pram. We then repeated the journey home later in the afternoon. "Just dropped by for tea dear" my Mother would say to her friend Anne.

When I was 6 and a half I transferred to the local State Primary, Chislehurst Road School. The difference between here and St Nicholas was somewhat of a culture shock. No neatly mown lawns or well appointed surroundings here. This was my first actual contact with the harsher side of life in the immediate post war years. An old Victorian building, peeling paintwork, outside toilets, an asphalt playground with many kids in it who were clearly from very deprived backgrounds, and for me – at that point in my life – some frighteningly large 10 and 11 year olds. None of these however, came close to arousing as much fear as Miss O'Neill.

There was a ditty going the rounds when I was at Primary school - "*Glory Glory Hallelujah, Teacher hit me with a ruler*" It had originated in the USA as a schoolboy song entitled "*Burning of the school*" and was sung to the tune of Battle Hymn of the Republic. The ensuing lines of the chorus of the US version go on "*so I stood behind the door with a loaded. 44, and she don't teach no more*" For the life of me I simply cannot remember the British version we sang!! Anyhow, there was no such escape from Miss O'Neill on the cards. She used a ruler on the knuckles with the same relish as a Samurai warrior might use his *katana* to fillet an enemy. But she got me through the 11 plus and into Grammar School. So it was constructive cruelty. Although I did not see it as such at the time!!

My Mother had also kept several of my Reports from the 4 years I was at Chislehurst Road. Year 1 shows me at Position 2 of 35 – astounding. Subsequent reports over the next 2 years show my Arithmetic, Reading and English were excellent, my History and Geography good, whilst at the same time my concentration levels could at times be below par. Bit of a dreamer. Art and Craft bored me, and I showed little interest in Physical Education – a proud tradition that I carried with me throughout my school days. Not that this stopped me roistering around with the best of them in the playground.

We would play hide and seek and "catch as catch can". When one of us was discovered / jumped on by the others he or she would shout the word "fain lites" meaning "I surrender". (I spell the word phonetically here, as I have never seen it written down. Nor have I been able to find it in even the multi dictionary set of the Oxford English Dictionary. Yet it was a word from my childhood that was widely used by 6 – 9 year olds.) Maybe it was simply the ideolect of the times long since discarded.

It was at Primary School of course that I had my first contact with girls. Brenda Williams, Geraldine Camoine – how do I remember these names?! And of course Shirley Wigley, the first love of my life when I was just 7. She was fair haired with freckles and pigtails. The very best thing that had ever happened to me up until then was when I was invited to her house for tea! Ever the little perfectionist, I remember coming away from her house worrying if I should have made such a pig of myself with the jam tarts. (*How these events stick in the mind for 60 years I have no idea*). But we slowly drifted apart – I think I got a train set for my birthday. I hope you have all had a good life since ladies.

I do recall that we all carried our own Autograph books to school and wrote in each others. I still remember that one of the girls (who it was escapes me now) had written "YY UR, YY U B, I C U R YY 4 Me ("*Who said modern teenagers invented text speak then?!!*). There were also several entries with versions of the "Roses are red –" variety. Puppy love.

Games aside, playtime at Chislehurst Road could also sometimes be hairy. The space in the playground was far too small for the number of pupils. Lots of bumping and shoving and general confusion. Once while playing cricket I stood too near the batsman and got knocked senseless when he swung the bat too hard. Especially worrisome had been if the two Council Estate boys from Homefield Rise were on patrol. You learnt to steer clear of Lenny and Pete, and of some of their cronies. They used to get into fights - they always won. Then one day the inevitable happened. Surrounded by a ring of cheering school boys they fought each other. The first time I ever saw blood.

Pete, the smaller one lost – it was a bit like a middleweight against a lightweight.

Like St Nicholas it wasn't.!

Proomas.

I should at this point mention how my surname was often cruelly and heartlessly mocked throughout my youth! Perhaps the most inventive example of this was when in November 1949 the first polar bear cub to be born in captivity in Britain arrived at London Zoo. It was given the name *Brumas*. I do not know why – but what I do know is that it caused minor havoc with my surname. I have always had problems with it. To this day I still get mail shots for Proon, Prume, Prune, Pron. The soubriquet of "Prunes and Custard" stayed with me throughout my youth. But from 1950 onwards I also acquired the monicker of *Proomas* after our ursine friend. Some of my closest mates – yes, you know who you are!! - still call me this on occasion.)

One of my best mates at Primary was Ian Cundell, a red headed boy of my age. We could often be found on summer evenings and at weekends climbing things and / or jumping off them. There were more than a few derelict building sites dotted around the town. Left empty since before the War, they had still not been re-developed over 10 years later. They served as ideal assault courses for 7 and 8 yr old boys. We ranged free like a pair of urchins from the supporting cast of Oliver in our patched short trousers, shirts made by our Mothers with the seams let out to allow for growth - and well darned socks.

We were the true sons of austerity. At least we both had Mothers who made us wash at nights. Scrubbing ourselves down with Lifebuoy soap. It had a pleasant scent to it - and contained carbolic acid as used in hospitals!

It was Ian who invented the game of Paratroopers. This entailed climbing up to the top of the coal bunker at the back of our house (around 5 ft off the ground) then vaulting across the intervening trellis in front of the flower bed on to the lawn. Around 12 feet. The object was to jump further than your opponent. It became quite popular with other class members, who would often pop round trying to beat the record. Still held I think by Ian.

I wonder whatever became of Ian?

CHAPTER 3

The essential difference between childhood in the 1940s and 1950s and childhood today can best be summed up in one word – Imagination. In a world without Computers, or the Internet, or Computer games, or I - Pods or I- pads or Kindles or Mobile phones or CDs or DVDs; or even Cassette players or Transistor radios or colour TV – all of which still lay more than 40 years into the distant future – we children had to rely much more on our imaginations. Another diversion for young kids like me at Primary school were the rub on transfers and wall decals from Walt Disney. Bedrooms were covered in them. Mickey Mouse mania reigned in those years.

In 2012 kids play War Games on their X Box. In our day we we played with actual toy soldiers, imagining the actions and fighting mock battles on the living room floor. Everything is in your face today in glorious Technicolour. There is no room for imagination or quiet contemplation. In 2012 there is enormous pressure on TV on kids from a young age from Media Advertising to "keep up with the Joneses" where their peers are concerned. To grow up as quickly as possible.

In the 1950s the Children's TV programming was minimal (*Muffin the Mule* and *Bill* and *Ben the Flowerpot men* - not forgetting *Little Weed* - was about as risqué as it got!) Today kids can watch adult programmes which only pay lip service to the supposed Nine PM Watershed. Childhood has been under merciless assault for decades now.

One thing in broadcasting that has not changed however is Radio drama. You still need to use your imagination even today. Our radio was a Bush model you fine tuned by hand to the station you wanted. It was housed in a cabinet the size of a small chest of drawers. Aside from the radio, books were perhaps our main source for escape from reality. So it was good my reading ability was ahead of my age group.

Reading was a vital skill to master in the early 1950s. For apart from the radio, there was little or no other extraneous diversion available to you as a child in your free time. "Biggles", "Swallows and Amazons", "The Famous Five" of Julian Dick Anne and Georgina and their dog Timmy – these are just some of the books that cascade back down from the past into the consciousness. There was a flickering black and white TV picture from the BBC, but very few people owned television sets (it was much later before we got one at home). That was the only channel available.

Then there were the comics. The 1950s was the golden age of British comics. There was "The Dandy" - how can one ever forget Desperate Dan and his Cow Pies, or Beril the Peril – or Korky the Cat?! Then there was "The "Beano", with the adventures of Denis the Menace and the Bash Street Kids with their dog Gnasher. Aided and abetted by Minnie the Minx – endless fun and joy.

Although I was far too young to even know the word at the time I read them, the real pleasure in these characters seems to me today that they were anarchic. Rebellious impish children kept in line by Schoolmasters in gowns wielding canes. This was why we kids really loved them so much. We wanted to be like them - even though we knew we shouldn't.

The "Eagle" was my favourite though. First published around my 7th birthday. it featured the adventures of "Dan Dare, Pilot of the Future". Dan led the first expedition to Venus in search of food to help feed humanity. The planet was inhabited by two races of people, the warlike *Treens* and the more friendly *Therons*. The *Treens* planned to take over their territory using as cannon fodder *Atlantine* slaves, serfs who had been captured from Earth centuries before. (*Knowledge of Venus was sketchy in 1951!*)

The Treens had a longer term objective of colonising Earth. This led eventually to the *Treen* wars as Dan and his loyal side-kick Digby battled in Deep Space with the square-headed green-skinned *Treens* and their leader the *Mekon* – a green puny creature with a huge head sitting cross legged on a gravity free floating platform that resembled a tea tray. Every issue of the Eagle held me in thrall. At school in more boring lessons I used to doodle the pitched battles as the "Black Cat" fighter drones of the Mekon attacked Dan Dare's Mother ship. Dan always triumphed.

But there was so much more than just Dan in the "Eagle". There were other features – who remembers PC 49, Harris Tweed the bumbling Detective, Jeff Arnold in his cowboy hat,. Then there was Macdonald Hastings, the Special Investigator appointed by the comic to perform acts of daring on behalf of their readers. He became the willing target in a knife thrower's act, a human firework - and even went to Canada and was chased by a Grizzly.

One of the more educational contributors to the Eagle was their resident boffin, Professor Brittain, who explained the actual workings of science and of many everyday things. He would cover particle theory, splitting the atom. Then there were the workings of a London Underground ticket machine, and the "cutaways" of the over and under tube tunnels for its trains. Later on there came the process of making ice cream and the workings of the Quebec Bridge. The best of all for me was

the cutaway diagram of the jet black "New Gas Turbine-Electric locomotive" - the first nail in the coffin of the Steam Age Magic!!

Last but not least, and in perhaps one of the first acknowledgements to the fair sex, the Eagle issued a sister comic "The Girl" You will have to ask Granny what was in that!

Collectors pay very large sums today for back copies of the "Eagle" apparently. Just a pity I cannot remember whatever became of mine. But never fear – I have just found out that original cartoons and articles from the comic have been reproduced and a retro- compilation album has recently. been published by Orion Books. I know this because my darling daughter, having read my proofs for this book, has just given it to me for my 70th birthday.!

To show just how popular these three comics were, and just how much influence they had on our young lives, each had an individual circulation in the early 1950s of well over One Million copies per issue. In addition each published a Christmas Annual that was at the top of every boy's list to Santa.

There was another Annual each Christmas – the Rupert the Bear Annual. Rupert was a cartoon strip created by a journalist on the *Daily Express* newspaper in 1920. It's original purpose apparently had been to attract readers from other papers. Rupert was an anthropomorphic bear who wore checked trousers and a jacket and lived with his parents in the fictional village of Nutwood. His friends were all animals in human form as well. As a young boy I always found the Rupert stories to have a strange, almost mystic quality about them.

He was always off on magical adventures to mythical lands. Always arriving at the drawbridges of far off castles not knowing what he would find on the other side of the walls. He had both an innocence and a world weariness about him. Looking back I think his creator saw the strip as an allegory of life. Rupert has certainly stood the test of time. His adventures are still chronicled daily in the paper after more than 90 years.

"Christmas comes but once a year, and when it does it brings good cheer" "runs the old adage. Good cheer was at a premium in the austerity years after the War, so everyone looked forward to the 25th December and Yuletide. Nanny Tanner always came to stay at Christmas. Phil and I shared my room. She had his. A week or so before the Happy Day Dad would bring home a fir tree in a pot to stand in the corner of the living room. He would bring the battered old cardboard box down from the attic, and we would hang battered tinfoil stars and old plastic baubles from its branches. A big gold star from some earlier era went on top.

The room itself was decorated with paper chains. Which we made by hand. You bought a big box of broad paper strips in various colours gummed at each end from the Woolworths in the High Street. You then folded one strip through and over another and licked the end so that it stayed in place – then continued this laborious process until a chain long enough to run the length of the room was produced which you pinned / tied to the wainscoting Repeat to criss cross every room – hours and hours of folding and licking.

Simple pleasures were paramount when that was all that was on offer. There was no tinsel in austerity Britain.

Then – finally – Christmas Eve arrived. As a child I remember Phil and I trying to stay awake at night to spot Santa coming down the chimney of the fireplace in my bedroom, and wondering if the dying embers in the grate would set fire to his beard. Mum and Dad would hang a clean white pillowcase at the end of our beds for Santa to fill with presents. In our house we opened presents after breakfast – or at 5 AM in the morning depending whether or not Phil and I could contain our excitement. Fat chance.

In the pillowcases there would be tangerines, nuts, presents wrapped in white tissue paper (there were no fancy "Festive Wrappings" available in post war Britain) The Annuals were there, and if you were really lucky Santa would have brought you a Hornby Dublo train set. Sometimes there might be a Meccano set, strips of shaped metal with holes that you could screw together with silvery screws to make all sorts of different structures such as houses, ships and many others.

Or there might be one of the latest brightly coloured Dinky model cars. An "Airfix" kit of a Spitfire or a Messerschmidt 109 might also have figured from the early 50s. (Completed kits of Spitfires hung by strings from a million boys' bedroom ceilings in those days.) One time I got a red Maserati racing car Dinky toy, another time a fire engine. Then there were jigsaw puzzles, tin whistles, drums, sets of coloured pencils – simple pleasures by today's consumerist standards. Sheer bliss by ours at the time.

One of the earliest presents I remember getting – I must have been around 5 or 6 – were a large spinning top painted in bright colours where you had to pump the handle in the middle up and down to set it going. I needed both hands to get it going. It played a tune as it whizzed round. The other was a kaleidoscope – the shifting colours and shapes as you turned the knob at the top were truly wondrous.

After breakfast we would get into our Sunday Best clothes – mostly surviving from before the War years where my parents were concerned – wrap up warmly against the winter chill, then go to All Saints for the Christmas Morning service and the Carol Concert. Then came Christmas Dinner. Roast turkey or chicken with all the trimmings, followed by Christmas Puddings with mince pies and custard. The one day of the year when no expense – or rationing points - were spared.

The Christmas Puddings were always home made. So were the mince pies. Children across Britain would watch as the rich mixtures of fruit, sweet mincemeat, peel and other ingredients for the pudding were mixed in a bowl by their Mothers, waiting for the moment when she would let them stir it as well, then lick the spoon. (Children today do not know what they are missing - you cannot do this with a ready made pudding from Sainsburys) A silver sixpenny piece would sometimes be put in the pudding mixture for some lucky diner to find.

We ate until we went pop, as Nanny Tanner used to say – before sitting down as loyal subjects of the Empire to listen to the King on the radio. In the evenings the boxes of Dates and the walnuts appeared. Mum and Dad would sip sherry or have a whisky. Phil and I would go to bed tired out, with cheeks red from excitement. Christmas is never the same when you are an adult. Also, in those days it did not start in the shops in September!

*

Often when children of my era went to bed another source of entertainment awaited us - the Cat's Whisker radio. As a young lad I used to listen to mine under the blankets in my bedroom on cold winter nights, the embers of the coal fire glowing in the fireplace in the corner. The forerunner to the transistor of later days, the Cat's Whisker, also known as a crystal detector, was a thin wire that lightly touched a crystal of a semi conducting mineral to form a crude rectifier. It was the earliest form of semi-conductor diode.(*I have no idea what any of this means, I just looked it up on the internet.*) All I did know was that if you tuned the very basic dial fitted to the small square gunmetal grey box to the right wavelength and radio station you could get Radio Luxembourg, with cutting edge pop music and its inchoate advertising for soap powders: and for the apparently famous "Racing Tipster" Horace Bachelor of Keynsham near Bristol.

Only much later did I find out what a tipster did. Until the early 1960s there were no High Street Betting shops or Off Course Bookmakers. The only places in Britain you could bet – legally - on a horse race were at the Race Courses themselves. This ensured that the attendances at Race meetings were huge. But it also meant that there was little or no pre-race intelligence on the field. Tipsters would provide racegoers with "dead certs" for cash upfront.

The most famous of all racing tipsters in the 40s and 50s, who most definitely did NOT need to advertise on the radio, was the larger than life character of *Ras Prince Monolulu*. He claimed to be an African chief, hence Prince, but his real name was Peter Carl Mackay, born the illegitimate son of a racehorse trainer on the island of St Croix in the West Indies in 1880. A huge black man, who often wore a feathered headdress, he had been married 5 times.

A celebrity in his own right, an associate of Royalty, and a legend of the Turf, his battle cry was "I gotta horse!" He had made his reputation at the Derby in 1920, when he personally pocketed £8,000 betting on the winner – this represented a huge sum of money in those days.

*

From the early 50s on the height of an evening's clandestine listening for me though was *"The Goon Show"* on the BBC. "The craziest and most madcap programme ever to be broadcast anywhere ever" as it was once described with no great insight by someone in the Radio Times.

With episodes entitled such as "The Kippered Herring Gang," The Flying Saucer Mystery "and" The Great Ink Drought of 1902" it featured 30 minutes of the adventures of Neddy Seagoon, with his nemesis Hercules Grytpype-Thinne, a cad and conman who was always trying to cheat him and often called him a "silly twisted boy". Others featuring in this madcap show included Eccles, Bluebottle, Minny Bannister, Henry Crun, General Cash my Check. These characters were all created and performed by Michael Bentine, Spike Milligan, Peter Sellers and Harry Secombe.

Although TV had been around since the late 1930s (with a 7 year hiatus for the War years), BBC Radio remained the only dominant broadcasting medium until the late 1950s. There were three main channels, the Home Service, the Light Programme and the Third Programme (Radio 4, Radio 2 and Radio Three today). The Light programme broadcast all the popular shows. Maybe the most popular of all in the post war years right up until 1967 was *"Have a go"* presented by Wilfred Pickles. This was an early form of quiz show where couples competed for prizes.

Pickles was a Yorkshireman and during the war became the very first BBC Newsreader with a regional accent. Apparently he had been selected so that his broad Yorkshire could not be imitated by the Nazis during the war if they made a false trans-mission. He would ask every couple on his show who came on the stage "Are yer courting?" His wife Mabel assisted him on the show, and if contestants won a prize Wilfred would say triumphantly "Give em the mooney Mabel"

The Light Programme also had a whole string of (yes you got it, "light hearted") programmes. Maybe the one with the great-est longevity was "Workers Playtime", appearing each day at lunchtime every day Monday to Friday. It ran from 1941 to 1967. The programme came live daily from a different factory somewhere in the UK (this of course was in the days when Britain still had enough Manufacturing Industry to provide a new venue every day!)

Big names appeared on it. Many had learned their trade in the Music Hall tradition. Comics almost always portrayed themselves as working class "Jack the lads "or "cheeky chappies. "as they were known. Even though some were middle class and the odd one upper crust –"it was not the done thing for a chap to tell jokes on stage, old man."

There was Arthur Askey, the original "Cheeky Chappy," Ted Ray, Tommy Trinder, Frankie Howerd, Peter Sellers, Charlie Chester -. even Morecambe and Wise!! Bringing up the rear came the zany Max Wall – and the raciest of them all, Max Miller (although his bluest material was reserved for later in the day). He was once banned from the BBC for several years after repeating his little ditty "When roses are red they are ready for plucking, when girls are 16 they are ready for —ing. "He left the last word hanging, but everyone of course knew what it was. This had created a huge scandal in the 1950s (although as most people had known what he meant, this was just another example of the hypocrisy of the age)

Even though in the 1950's they were all huge stars., by and large their material would have been seen as pretty lame today in the current climate of Alternative comedy (definition: *something that isn't funny"*). Although a few did go on to become even greater names in ensuing decades: performers such as Frankie Howerd, Tony Hancock and Peter Sellers learned their trade on the Light Programme.

Morning programmes were aimed almost exclusively at housewives, who did not go out to work in those days. "Housewives Choice "would kick off proceedings around 9, followed by "Music while you work". (*There were no feminists in the*

1950s!) Then there was "Mrs Dale's Diary". The first serial on British Radio, it was about a Doctor's wife. It ran from 1948 to 1969 – and was of course then promptly replaced by "The Archers."

(I continued to enjoy comedy on the Light Programme well into the 1960s. With "Comedy Half Hours" of which there were many. "The Navy Lark" with Jon Pertwee, "Hancock's Half Hour" with the brilliant but inevitably doomed Tony Hancock and his nemesis played by Sid James: the man with the dirtiest laugh in Show Business. There was "Life with the Lyons," "Around the Horne" with Kenneth Horne and an all star cast – the list was almost endless. Bringing up the rear was "Whacko!" starring Jimmy Edwards, a big lump of a man with a huge handlebar moustache who played a cane - happy Headmaster.)

For the rest of the time we all had to invent our own amuse-ment through our imagination. From the late 40s onwards we lived out of doors in the summer, coming back just for meals. For the reasons already explained, we could roam far and near and be completely safe. Sometimes it was just locally – up Stanley, continue on down St Kilda Road to Broxbourne Common to climb the trees and play ball.

Other times, we went down Keswick Road to Chislehurst Rd, across the common and up Sandy Lane to the Mount, an exposed sandy hillside on the way to Poverest Recreation ground. We would then race each other to the top, the winner shouting triumphantly *"I'm the King of the Castle, get down you dirty rascal!"* The Mount was also ideally suited for a game of Cowboys and Indians. On the Rec itself we actually did play football with sweaters as goal posts.

Occasionally while climbing trees one of us would fall off a branch: maybe sometimes even fractured a limb. I never heard of anyone dying. Plaster casts were a badge of honour – although I must say that happily I never needed to wear one. But nobody ever called Social Services or muttered about child neglect. In those days adults still had a sense of proportion about such things.

After all it had been less than 10 years since most Fathers of young children had been fighting the Nazis. Most had seen comrades die in front of them. What were a few broken bones? The "Blame" culture we all live under today would not appear until the late 1990s. Another nail in the coffin of childhood. Another triumph for the lawyers.

Frankly there is just one respect in which parents of young children today should really worry about the safety of their offspring – Road Traffic. Otherwise they should allow them free rein. If a child does not grow up to be able to recognise and cope with risks or dangers how will they cope with the real World?

The Flicks

Of course, for both children and adults the main source of escapism in the 1940s and 1950s had been the Motion Picture. The 1940s have always been considered to have been the Golden age of cinema. Or the ""flicks"as we used to call them then. Every town had at least one cinema, probably more than one. We had two, the larger being the Commodore, which could seat around 800. It had its own Commissionaire dressed in a white uniform and cap with gold epaulettes and a white lanyard and a gold trimmed peaked cap.

Most cinemas and all of the big London stores had *Commissionaires* in those days. They were all ex Army, many of them senior NCOs. They often wore their medals on their chests. They also tended to be tall and on the burly side, so were perhaps the first generation of the modern bouncer – although they would have been appalled I am sure to think of themselves as such.

The chap who owned the Commodore had the house two doors down from us in Stanley Road. I remember only a tall slim rather dour looking man. And that he had a Swimming pool in his back garden; unheard of in the austere 1950s. He did not have much to be miserable about – in 1946 cinema audiences had stood at 1.64 Billion.

It was estimated just after the War that 80% of the population had gone to the Cinema at least once a year. He must have been raking it in hand over fist. (The 1946 audience figures were the highest they would ever reach. By 1956 they had slumped by almost 40% - television had arrived for real.) Coronation Street began at the end of 1961 – and the rest is history.

The other local cinema was The Palace – formerly the Carlton - a somewhat oxy-moronic name given that it was fondly known by the population of Orpington at large as the Flea Pit or the Bug Hutch. With some justification. It had no commissionaire outside – a street cleaner might have been more appropriate. The Germans had tried to destroy it in 1945 - but had sadly missed!

The Embassy in Petts Wood was the biggest in the area, seating almost 1,300. In the early 50s the Embassy began to hold a special Children's programme of films on Saturday mornings. I used to go regularly, catching the train one station down the line to Petts Wood. The Cinema was right next to the station. I would usually meet kids I knew in the foyer.

For the show you could perm any of several from the following – Tex Ritter, the Lone Ranger, Hopalong Cassidy, Roy Rogers, Tarzan, Flash Gordon against Ming the Merciless,

Lassie and others I cannot even recall. There were Disney cartoons – Donald Duck and Goofy seemed to feature strongly – and my very favourite comedy act "The Three Stooges". Moe, the ringleader, Larry and Shemp – they always had me in stitches. I think the price of entry for this cornucopia of entertainment was a tanner (six old pennies – 2.1/2p.

There were few other diversions for us kids in those austere years. According to the definitive work on the subject of British confectionery, the website Sweet and Nostalgic, we British spend over £3 Billion p.a on *sweeties*. A visit to the site is a trip down memory lane for children of the 40s and 50s. There had been an almost complete bar on the production of confectionery during the war years Sweets contain sugar of course and this had been one of the foodstuffs most strictly rationed.

Then in 1948 they began to creep back into the shops. Who can forget Fry's Chocolate Creams, the Great Granddaddy of them all, first introduced in 1866! Rolos and Smarties from 1935 are still with us today. Polo Mints arrived in 1948, as did Fruit Spangles. These were our staple sweets. Bounty bars arrived in 1951 and are still going strong today. If you like coconut – not me, yukk! Now you have a hundred different varieties of *choccies* – and you have growing obesity in children and adults.

Even austerity can have health benefits.

CHAPTER 4

By the beginning of the 1950s, Britain had been at a low ebb. There had been rationing for nearly a decade, and there had been very slow progress in rebuilding our bomb - shattered cities. GDP hit an all time low – nearly half a million lives had been lost to the work force, and Industry during the war years had been skewed heavily towards armaments and food production. So in 1951, in an effort to build up national morale and bang the drum for British exports, the Festival of Britain was opened on the South Bank of the Thames - on the site that now contains the Royal Festival Hall and the National Theatre.

One of its main protagonists had been Herbert Morrison a Labour MP and former Mayor of London. He described it as "the British showing themselves to themselves, and to the world "Red double decker buses – the most powerful symbol of London there has ever been – were despatched to Europe as Ambassadors for the Exhibition to visit Scandinavia, Germany France and the Netherlands. They contained delegations from leading British manufacturing companies. Apparently they did over 4,000 miles without breaking down. Over 6 million people visited the Exhibition site and satellite sites in major British cities. It was adjudged to have been a great success for the Labour Government of Clement Attlee.

So when the country returned Churchill and a Conservative Government at the end of 1951, it was rapidly demolished.

There may have been a sense of common purpose in the country: but Politics as ever was Politics.

My parents took me to the Festival Exhibition in the summer of 1951. I remember quite clearly as an 8 yr old child how exciting the whole thing seemed in those dark days of austerity. The symbol for the Festival was the Skylon, the elongated cone shaped futuristic "needle "installation at its heart. But what really impressed was the "Dome of Discovery". Covering an area the size of a football pitch it was at that time the largest dome in the World. Inside it was almost 90 feet high, with three separate galleries containing dozens of montages celebrating British pre-eminence in Discovery, Exploration (large areas of the globe in 1951 were still coloured pink on a map) and in areas such as medicine. It was meant I think the to symbolise the very nature of the Universe with Britain at its heart. As a small boy I found it mind blowing in its vastness.

But perhaps my most vivid and lasting recollection of our trip to the Festival of Britain had been the view from the train after we passed Hither Green on the way to London Bridge. I had been horrified by what I saw. The devastation wreaked by German bombers in the Blitz. Hardly a building remained uns-carred. Bare unsupported walls leaning at crazy angles loomed over vast open spaces strewn with rubble and bomb craters. Many of the buildings left standing were mere shells open to the elements. Whole areas had quite simply been flattened. How anyone could have survived this I couldn't imagine.

It had not been the first time I had travelled to London on the Orpington Line. But I had been too young at those times to be affected by the bomb craters. In Mother's papers I found a picture of me, in a thick winter overcoat, feeding the pigeons in Trafalgar Square. From the picture I must have been around 3. I also vividly remember a particular visit my Mother and I made to Hamleys in Regent Street, the most famous toy store in London and possibly the world (my wife and I bought toys for our two in Hamleys three decades later.). As we were walking up the winding central staircase from the Ground Floor Mother suddenly stopped and looked across at some-body walking down past us. "Ooh look dear" she said "that's Bonar Colleano"

This meant nothing at all to me at the time, nor for many more years. Yet it is strange how some events just stick in the mind – so much so that I recently looked him up. Turns out that he had been an American Music Hall performer and Film star who lived in London, and was tragically killed in a road accident in 1958.

Rover

When I was about seven another new member of the family arrived. Rover came into our lives. A wriggling ball of jet black fur under Dad's raincoat., he was possibly the daftest example of a daft breed there has ever been – a black Labrador Retriever. Any parent seeking the right dog as a pet for the family should consider this breed first. They have the sweetest nature, are perfect with children – as my brother and I found out when we wrestled with him on the floor, pulling his ears and tail repeat-edly; or when he chased us around the garden, panting with his tongue lolling out; and when he jumped up and pressed his cold wet nose into our faces. We always said that if we were ever burgled, Rover would love the culprit into submission!

His main diet was tripe from the butcher – sheep intestines, the poorest dregs from a carcass but full of nutriment. This was not rationed as it was considered fit for animals only. The smell of Tripe boiling up in the cooking pot is one of the foulest imaginable. He supplemented his diet by wheedling tit bits out of us round the dinner table – and by stealth. Anyone who has had dogs will know that they will eat almost anything. Rover once ate an entire pack of butter, wrapping and all, that Mum had left on the kitchen table. We also gave him *Winalot* dog biscuits which provided the proper vitamins and trace elements for health and were good for his teeth. The combination sure seemed to be good for him – he ran all of us ragged most of the time.

As he left puppy hood behind him and grew into dog hood he took a gross exception for some reason to the Ginger cat next door, and began to wage an endless and ultimately fruitless war of attrition against it. The cat in turn used to sit on the top of the privet hedge and glare superciliously at him. Every time he lunged after the dastardly moggy it ran up a tree from which dizzy height it proceeded to mock him further. Rover would then beat a strategic retreat – often with two pinpricks of blood on his damp nose where the cat had swiped him on the way up the tree. This went on for years as I recall – the cat won every bout.

Never had a dog been better named. Once Rover had learned how to vault the privet – whilst still having no idea how to catch his feline tormentor – he was off. He would slip through next door's side entrance and then roam the district, sometimes staying out for several days at a time. To feed himself, he would sometimes drop round the yard at the back of the Butcher's in the High Street to pinch a juicy bone off the rack. In the end they just used to give him one. But being a black Labrador, and therefore a member of the most lovable breed known to man, he had quickly mastered the art of conning old ladies into feeding him.

He wore a collar with a dog tag so we would get calls from far and near from those he had conned. In those days the Police were responsible for stray dogs. So occasionally a concerned member of the public would find Rover and ring St Mary Cray Police station. (Probably just to get him out of their kitchen!) A nice Constable would then be despatched to take him to the police kennel where he usually got sausages for his tea.

Now Rover might have been daft, but like all animals where grub is concerned, he was not stupid. After this had happened a few times he decided that he would dispense with the middle-man. So when he was weary of roaming he would therefore just present himself at the Police station without human interven-tion. The lure of sausages would always be ultimately irresist-ible. He must have been largely responsible for the Kent Constabulary's total feed budget for stray animals. The local bobbies seemed to find this whole process hilarious, and made a great fuss of Rover – thus ensuring his continued visits and undivided attentions. Our dog must have spent almost as much time in Police custody as he did on the rug in front of the fire.

Rover lived to the age of 11. He was a much loved member of the family. We missed him terribly when he died – so much so in fact that Mum and Dad could not bear to have another dog. It was as Kipling puts it in his dictum: "Brothers and Sisters I bid you beware, of giving your heart to a dog to tear "He was very special.

Park Langley

They say that smells have the most powerful effect on the memory of any other stimuli. The smell of formaldehyde is one of the most pungent smells known to man. Once experienced it is always remembered. The smell of formaldehyde always evokes for me the visits I made with Dad at weekends and holi-days to the Wellcome Research Laboratories at Park Langley in Beckenham where he worked. In his lab there were always plenty of Petrie dishes filled with cultures growing on jelly. As a leading micro bacteriologist germs were his thing. The smell of formaldehyde was everywhere in the lab. Dad would try to explain in terms a seven or eight year old would understand which bacteria were which. He would also let me look at slides of various insects under his microscope. I soon learned to identify the stings of wasps from the stings of bees. Wasps' stings were smooth and retracted after piercing the skin. Bee stings were barbed – which means that when a bee stings the poor creature cannot retract the sting and will die. The antennae of beetles were my favourite – they looked almost extra-terrestrial under magnification.

Dad would also give me a guided tour of the extensive stables. These did not smell of formaldehyde but of dung and warm straw. They housed a a whole string of horses – all of them mares. But why were they there?

It was because since being founded in the 1880s by Henry Wellcome, BW by the 1940s had grown to become a world leader in the production of vaccines. This process was greatly assisted by the ladies in those stables – the brood mares into whose blood antibodies were injected and from whose blood and urine the pure proteins were then extracted that are essential for vaccine production. They were at that time perhaps the most valuable – and best looked after – horses on the planet.

My Father himself had always had doubts about immunisation. He had sat on the Government Immunisation Committee when it had been formed after the war, and counselled caution in mass immunisation programs. I also have the complete script of a talk he once gave on the subject on the BBC Radio Home Service (now Radio 4) In one sense he was over cautious. Although he died sadly early at the end of 1963 at the age of 57, and never lived to see them, his grandchildren have been immunised against the major childhood diseases and I can say happily that they never fell prey to them. Millions of others were immunised successfully as well. On the other hand, given the recent dispute over MMR vaccines and autism, maybe he had a point.

Burroughs Wellcome itself underwent a series of further mergers, with the Wellcome family finally selling out for a very great deal of money*, and eventually became part of the present day pharmaceutical giant Glaxo Smith Kline. I wonder if their shareholders realise just how much they owe to a group of brood mares in the stables at Park Langley.

*The majority of the proceeds from the sale of Wellcome were placed into the Wellcome Trust, based today in Euston Road in London. It has grown into one of the largest philanthropic organisations in the world, investing in advances in Medical Science. It is good to know that my Father played a role in that.

*

Scouting for Boys.

When I was eight I got my first woggle when I joined the Wolf Cubs. Every new recruit had to swear allegiance "to God and the King". (As the Jesuits said, "Give us the child until he is seven and we will give you the man") We met at the Church Hall just off the High Street. Where I also attended Sunday School every week.

Wolf pack leaders were almost always women, universally addressed as "Akela" - the name of the She Wolf in the Mowgli story by Rudyard Kipling. Thus began my 7 years + association with the Scouting movement. As cubs we went on field trips to places like Cudham and studied flora and fauna

We marched up and down in our tan coloured shirts with our scarves tucked into our woggles. We played tag in the Hall in the winter. What was inculcated into us at all times was that we must have a sense of duty towards our fellow man. That we must strive to be honest and honourable at all times. That we must be self reliant. These had been the principles on which

Baden-Powell had formed the Scouting Association after the Boer War, when Britain had still ruled over half the globe.

When I was 10/11 I transferred to the Big league - the Boy Scouts. This was much more interesting. We played British Bulldog in the Church Hall in the winter months – a cross between Rugby and wrestling. Two teams running at each other and colliding in the middle. We worked on qualifying for a wide range of badges which were then sewn on to our uniformed shirts. Field crafts of all types figured prominently. Also orienteering, map reading and other para military activities. All of this had been regarded as extremely character building in the spirit of Baden Powell.

In the Spring came Bob a Job Week. We would each go door to door in our own area of streets dressed in our uniforms offering to do odd jobs for a "Bob" or a shilling. Anything from weeding flower beds to walking dogs or cleaning windows. The point being that all proceeds went to charity.

This tradition died out in the 1990s when ' Elf and Safety, Social Services and all the massed ranks of the Nanny State decreed that young people were "at risk" knocking on strangers' doors. The fact that no young person from the Scouting Association in its entire 90 year history had ever been abused, sexually or otherwise, nor abducted, robbed, attacked or put upon in any way whilst offering to do Bob a Job door to door did not of course bother the zealots in their ivory towers. I think that the thing that must have nauseated these nannies of the State more than anything else about the Scouting movement had been its doctrine of "Self Reliance". *Self reliance – where does that leave our jobs then?* they must have thought.

Our Scout Master was a young chap, Brian Blisset, who eventually went on to become the General Manager of Orpington Hospital. He was a very friendly and enthusiastic chap who oversaw the building of the new Scout Hut in Goddington Lane. There is one thing relating to Brian of which many of our scout troop, myself included, are not proud of in retrospect.

He had as a pet a Saluki hound, a large long golden haired, spindly legged animal. As a breed they are renowned for their neurotic temperament. If you crept up on the dog then shouted "Boo" very loudly right behind it, the poor animal would jump several feet into the air. There was an ongoing competition to see who could make the dog jump the highest. This is of course the sort of cruel thing that young adolescent males find excruciatingly funny – and try to forget when they grow into adulthood.

The best thing of all for me about being a Boy Scout was the camping. Sleeping under canvas on a ground sheet, wrapped in a sleeping bag, there is little that compares with the fresh smell of a morning dew on grass in summer right next to your nostrils. We made a crude form of bread by mixing unleavened flour with water and forming them into crude patties that we then stuck on sticks and baked over a camp fire as billy cans of baked beans and others filled with water for the tea were suspended bubbling on a tripod over the flames.

One camping trip in particular sticks in my mind. One summer – I must have been 13/14 years old – we went to a National Scouting Camp Centre in Lyndhurst in the New Forest. There were lots of high jinks – especially concerned with evening attempts to break into the "High Security" compound housing the Girl Guides camp site. Seldom had a compound been more stoutly defended. I recall that one of the Senior Ranger Scouts tried to drive in in the troop Land Rover, but was swiftly sent on his way by the stout defenders. Fearsome women they were, the Guide leaders.

We were camped by a slow running stream where we washed ourselves and our cooking pots and brushed our teeth every day.

Until one day, foraging upstream, we found the decomposing carcass of a New Forest pony that had clearly not died the day or even the week before. After that we drew water from the taps provided. Sadly it was not my only encounter with New Forest ponies at that camp. A few days later I made the one mistake people who work with horses always counsel against – I walked up close behind one. As its back legs flew out and I sailed backwards through the air I vowed I would never walk up behind another equine creature again! My midriff was sore for several weeks.

On other evenings we would sit around a small bonfire singing the famed scouting song – "Ging gang goolie goolie goolie goolie goolie, ging gang goo, ging gang goo. Hayla, hayla shayla, hayla hayla hayla hoo" What do the words mean? They mean absolutely nothing. They are pure gibberish. The song was said to have been written by Baden Powell at the first Scouting Jamboree after the First World War in 1920. He deliberately chose gibberish so that it could be sung by scouts from foreign lands who might not speak English.

With good reason as it turned out - for despite the fact that the Scouting movement had been formed with the preservation of the British Empire in mind, there are still today Scout Associations with associated Scout troops in 23 separate nations across the Globe. In Israel, in Japan and in Brazil to name but three. My first hand experience of this came a few years ago when I flew into Terminal 3 at Heathrow to find the Arrivals and Baggage Halls teeming with literally hundreds of Boy Scouts in full uniform from several nations – some from Canada, a lot from Japan. They were on their way to the latest International Scouting Association Jamboree held in Essex.

So all of those on the politically correct Left in the UK today who pour scorn on the personal qualities of self reliance, duty to others, honour and respect for their leaders might just like to bear that fact in mind. Many other nations still hold Baden Powell's virtues in great esteem Even if you cynically deride them so as to promote your own Political Agenda.

Sadly, things are very different now, apparently, in today's modern British Scouting Association. For one thing, as I write this in April 2012, certain senior members of the Scouting Association in the UK are questioning the wording of the Oath of Allegiance. They think the God bit will offend entrants of other faiths, and that the Monarch bit is outmoded in the modern world. I would remind them that Members of Parliament have to swear allegiance to the Crown and they might just be a tad more important to the nation than the Head of the Essex Scouts. (*Some of them, anyhow. Maybe*).

The Scouting Association already has previous in this. I understand they have since dispensed with the traditional chanting of "Dyb Dyb Dyb" or "Do your best" and our traditional rote response "Dob Dob Dob" - "Do our best". Yes, Baden-Powell had formed the Scouting movement after his experiences in the Boer War along military lines. Britain at that time had still ruled half the Globe. Many Scouts who went through the early Scout movement would eventually be posted to stations around the world either as military personnel or as District Commissioners and Colonial Administrators.

So to teach them self reliance, field craft, group discipline and respect for superiors at an early age had in his view been vital. But what is wrong in inculcating a sense of duty to others and group discipline into adolescents? *(Lord only knows what a better place this sceptred isle would be today if the Education system did it. Or rather, if it allowed Teachers to do it))*

Now I see that the position of Chief Scout of the Scouting Association is filled by a Television personality; a self-publicist who has been presenting "Adventure in the Wild" programs on

Cable TV for a number of years. A man who, it has been widely reported in the Press, feigns to live rough in tents in winter on screen, yet actually buggers off to a nice cosy Hotel room once the cameras have stopped filming. If this is true, what does THAT teach boys about self reliance, honour, duty and respect? There have also been accusations in the Press recently that he is exploiting his – honorary – position as Chief Scout so as to market his own range of "survival" and field and camping equipment.

In any event, the whirring sound Scouts may sometimes hear at nights will be Baden-Powell turning in his grave.

CHAPTER 5

The Scout Hut in Goddington Lane served a dual purpose. The Orpington Band rehearsed there on a Monday evening. The main date in the calendar every year for them was Whitsun weekend when they provided the live music for the Orpington Fête at Goddington Park. This was for all of us one of the very few bright rays of sunshine in the otherwise deep gloom of the austerity years.

It was always opened by some dignitary nobody had ever heard of – well I hadn't anyhow and Dad said he hadn't either! I think there may have been an actor one year, but if so then his identity is lost now in the mists of time. There were fair rides, donkey rides for Phil, coconut shies, hoop la stalls, shooting ranges - even a troupe of clowns. Stalls selling Tizer and lemonade for the kids and beer for the Dads. For a few hours at least everyone forgot rationing and hardship (well the adults anyhow - we kids did not know any other lifestyle)

Ah Tizer – by early 1950 it had already been around 25 years. It was the citrus soft drink of choice for millions of us kids in the 40s and 50s – until we graduated to something stronger. Coca cola gradually supplanted it as the 50s dragged on. Understand it may be making a comeback.

Another good day out was the Annual Open Day at the Fire Station. Every small boy – and many much bigger ones – dream of driving a big red monster to a call out. In those days they still rang a bell mounted outside on a stand by the passenger seat. This was the only warning to traffic they had in those days that they were coming through: no sirens, no blue lights. Traffic volumes were still very low, so they could be heard. We would be allowed to sit behind the wheel, clamber on to the back and stand on the – bottom – rung of the ladder. Magic. They also had a Tower out the back where they practised rope rescues. No boys – or Dads - allowed.

I must have been 6 or 7 when I first went to a Brigade Open Day. Less than 10 years before many units from the Kent Brigade had been fire fighting during the Blitz in the East End of London alongside other units from all over Britain. There are several references in the National Fire Brigades Roll of Honour to Medals being given for bravery to Kent fire crews. Firemen have always been brave men, and always will be. When their Superiors allow them to be.

How different things are today, when the same breed of brave men are ordered by their superiors NOT to proceed with rescues until they have done a "Risk Assessment". Good job they hadn't had Risk Assessments in 1940. The entire City of London would have been consumed in the flames. "Lions led by donkeys" was how British troops were described in the First World War. The same could be seamlessly applied to UK Firemen in the 21st Century.

If Political Correctness doesn't eventually destroy the fabric of our Society, our Bulldog spirit, then 'Elf and Safety surely will.

Hands across the Ocean

The special relationship between the UK and the US had been at its zenith in the War years. Before Pearl Harbour, while the US was still officially neutral, Roosevelt had provided warships for the Royal Navy under the Lend Lease scheme - and throughout the hostilities those Brits with relatives/friends in the States were kept well provisioned with food parcels.

My Aunt Doreen, my Mother's sister, had emigrated to California as a young woman in the mid 1930s. There she met and then married my Uncle Pic, who was the Vice President of the Standard Oil Company of New Jersey – or Exxon as it is now known. Auntie sent regular food parcels throughout the war years. One thing I did not know until Mother died in December 2010 is that her husband, Uncle Pic – whom I never met – had also sent me via my parents a small silver Christening mug It would not have been possible to buy one of those in Britain in 1943. Mum, being a War wife, had obviously squirrelled this away at the time and had probably forgotten all about it long before she died. It now has pride of place on our mantelpiece.

The food parcels from LA continued after the war. She also sent me one Christmas a battery powered motor launch she had bought at a Toy store there. It barely fitted into the pillowcase. I took it straight off to the Ponds behind what is now the Churchill Centre in Bromley, some 5 miles away, and sailed it proudly around. The boat must have felt at home – the box in which it came carried the words "Made in Bromley Kent, United Kingdom" (This was not as crazy as it sounds. British Industry had been geared up almost exclusively for the Export Trade in the immediate post war years. The Government needed the Foreign Currency.)

Aunt Dee was widowed in the 1950s, and remarried my Uncle Art. Who then sadly spent several years drinking and gambling away most of the money Pic had left her. After divorcing him she continued to live in LA in reduced circumstances before finally returning to the UK in the early 70s to live with Mother in Orpington. Like many sisters before them, they fought like cat and dog all the time - until Mother remarried in 1977 and moved to Hastings. Dee followed and settled into a flat there for the rest of her days.

The Retail experience

Another thing that I clearly remember while growing up was going shopping with Mum. I have been trying to remember the choice of shops in Orpington High Street. There was Cullens the Grocers, Mac Fisheries, David Greig the Butchers, Timothy Whites the Chemists (none of these chains any longer exists); an Ironmongers, several shoe shops. Freeman Hardy and Willis was the largest – it was where Mum took me to buy school shoes. It was fun – they had a machine that I guess was an X Ray that showed how well shoes fitted the bones of your feet. Doubtless banned by Health and Safety a lot of years later.

There were several bakers shops; the one at the bottom of Knoll Rise had the Children's Library above it. Spent a lot of time in there I did. There were Mens and Ladies clothiers, drapers and jewellers. Further down there was the Music shop where a few years later I would ask them to play a particular 78 vinyl, then go into a booth and listen to it with headphones without obligation. (Been to your local music shop recently? You have to find the CD you want from a rack of thousands, then queue to pay for it while a disinterested assistant with acne ignores you) There were Drapers, lots of smaller establishments selling anything and everything. There was the ubiquitous Woolworths, with it's wooden floors and piles of sweets just inside the entrance to tempt us kids. What there was not in the British High Street of the early 50s was a Supermarket. Supermarkets did not come on the scene until a bit later.

Then there the two "Greengrocers and Fruiterers". Their wares were displayed in wooden crates and you picked what you wanted. The vegetables were sold loose, often with the earth from which they had been pulled still on them. Potatoes, cabbage and carrots were the mainstays in everyone's diet. Then came beans and peas. Not the pre- frozen, pre -washed peas in plastic bags everyone pulls out of the deep freeze at the Supermarket today, but peas *au naturel* – still encased in their thick green pods. The more pliant the pods the fresher the pea, as the pods hardened and turned a shade of yellow the older they got. Unsurprisingly, they were always the ones left at the end of the day.

(One of my delights as a young child was preparing the peas before Mum cooked them. You split the pods lengthways, and inside you found two rows of peas attached to a central spine. You scooped them out with your fingers straight into a colander for washing. The whole process was called "shucking the peas". No idea what the derivation is.)

Fruit was mainly apples, pears and plums. Home grown. Imported fruit such as Oranges and tangerines were often only available at Christmas time. Bananas imported from the West Indies were only available from time to time - and sold out in minutes as word got round that a particular shop had had a delivery. *But on the plus side, our entry to the EU was still almost 3 decades away - so bananas could still be any shape you liked!!*

There is still the series of alleyways, 60 years on, that take you all the way down to the High Street. First you take the long narrow sloping alley from Stanley Rd that leads down to the bottom of Oatfield Road. (This alley was narrow and unlit at night. Even as a teenager I used to get that momentary atavistic frisson of danger we all inherit from the days of the cavemen; that one which forces you sometimes even against your will to look over your shoulder every so often to assure yourself that there is nobody – or nothing – behind you.) Then we took the second alley down to Vinson Close and the third shorter one down to the High Street past the side of *Meakers, the Gentleman's Outfitters.*

Cullens the grocers was opposite Meakers. It was everything the modern Supermarket isn't. Most basics – eg sugar, flour, tea, Lux soap flakes – were served from deep containers with the kind of large scoops you only find now in pet food shops. Butter was served in pats with a large spatula. All were sold by weight and packed with no wrapping, other than greaseproof paper where appropriate, into separate plain brown paper bags by a courteous friendly and most of all INTERESTED assistant in an apron. Ham and tongue were sliced on a bacon slicer and also wrapped in greaseproof paper. Fray Bentos Corned beef all the way from Montevideo was sold tinned. "Robertsons" jams and "Branston Pickle" in jars. That was it where packaging was concerned. Glass, paper, tins, greaseproof. Nobody had heard of recycling 60 years ago. Although you could get money back on empty bottles for re-use. Most assistants had to be numerate, and be able to do addition and long multiplication in their heads (just as well, as the first pocket calculators would not be invented for another 25 years)

As far as I remember there was no such thing as pre packaged meals in the immediate post war years. The woman of the house cooked everything herself. As meat was in very short supply, a lot of pastry and dumplings went in to the mix to make up bulk. Other times there would be fish dishes. Mum cooked a mean apple pie, with the fruit from the garden, and steak and kidney pie - when the meat was available.

Aside from that meals were pretty basic and improvised around what was available. There was no need for sell by dates on any food item – the last line of defence was the nose. Once at home, if perishables smelt bad you threw them away. Except that in the days of rationing food always ran out long before it ever had the chance to go bad.

The same rules applied to fish from the Fishmonger and Meat from the Butchers. Bread was always baked fresh on site at the

Bakers and I cannot remember there being ANY sliced bread on sale at all. Then there was Spam; one of the mainstays of the diet for British fighting men in World War Two and the staple "delicacy" in the diet for many millions of British families in the rationing years. A mix of pressed pork and pressed ham with added salt and water in a tin, I can recommend slices of Spam fried in a pan and known as spam fritters. Delicious.

Well, they seemed delicious at the time. (Quite frankly, you ate what you could get and were grateful even in the 7 – 8 years after the war) Another of the "delicacies" I do remember were Kraft cheese slices. Put into sandwiches with slices of tomato. The basic sandwich of the era. Yummy.

Most of the shops had young lads with bicycles with large baskets fitted to the handlebars who would deliver to your home. One or two shops actually had a van. What else did all these establishments have in common?. Personal Customer service with a smile. Every shopkeeper knew most of his customers by name, knew their favourite items – which cut of meat, which type of fish, Brussels sprouts or cabbage - and had time to pass the time of day with them.

(*Compare this with today - when did you last get service like that from your local Supermarket or from the other semi-monopolistic retailers in our High Streets and Shopping Malls? The persons on the checkout there do not know you from Adam, most do not care, and are not interested in anything other than your credit card details. They in turn are now being replaced by Self Service checkouts – so soon there will be absolutely no level of personal service at all left in any of our shops.*)

As I keep telling you – life was so very different then.

CHAPTER SIX

The Coronation.

June 2ndrd 1953 was one of the most historic days of the 20th century. The Coronation of Queen Elizabeth 11 took place in Westminster Abbey. It was the first major international event ever to be shown on live Television anywhere in the world. But very few people had TV then. Her Majesty wore a white dress designed by Norman Hartnell. It had been embroidered with the thistle of Scotland and the leek of Wales. It also bore the symbols of the countries of the Commonwealth – the Wattle of Australia, the Protea of South Africa, the New Zealand fern, the Canadian Maple leaf and two Lotus flowers for India and Ceylon (now Sri Lanka).

None of these had much effect on the flickering black and white TV screen. Happily though, the ceremony itself had been filmed in glorious Technicolour, and was shown in cinemas across the land a few days afterwards. I went to see it on the big screen at the Commodore cinema in the High Street. I remember the excitement to this day. Aside from anything else it was the first film in colour that I had ever seen.

In fact there had been a double feature at the Commodore that afternoon. 4 days before the Coronation, on May 29th 1953, Edmund Hillary and Sherpa Tensing had made the first successful ascent of Mount Everest. The expedition had also been filmed in colour. So after the Queen came the Kiwi and Sherpa show. What a fantastic double bill that had been for a 10 year old – a real feast for the eye steeped in history and tradition - and in courage.

(My future pal, Howard, at the age of 9, had had a particular reason for attending the Ceremony. He and his elder brother Mike had been choirboys in the Chapel Royal St James's Palace Choir, known as the Queen's Choir. The story of how and why they had got there is told later in this book).

At the end of the performance, the audience had stood to attention as the National Anthem was played on the cinema loudspeakers. This had not been a special event to celebrate the Coronation – in those days theatre and cinema audiences across the land would stand to attention at the end of EVERY performance while the Anthem was played. The only difference from then on would be that it was "God Save the Queen" rather than "God Save the King."

DNA

The Coronation was indeed a majestic pageant of British power and influence. It was a very important event. But it had been a month earlier, on 25th April, that perhaps the Number One Most Important Discovery ever made by Mankind was detailed in an article by two leading Biologists, Francis Crick, an Englishman, and James Watson, an American, in the Magazine "*Nature*". Entitled "*Molecular Structure of Nucleic Acids – a structure for Deoxyribose Nucleic Acid*" it announced their discovery of the correct helix structure of human DNA. This won them the Nobel prize for Medicine in 1962. In the past 60 years their initial mapping of DNA has led to countless medical advances and to the construction of the Human genome.

Empire

In the early 1950s our new Queen had still ruled over a truly global British Empire. As Viscount Field Marshal Montgomery, the hero of El Alamein and second in command to Eisenhower on D Day was reported as saying in the early 50s - "Being born British gives you first place in the lottery of life" It really was an Empire on which the sun never set.

In addition to the by now self governing "Senior" members of the Commonwealth – Canada, Australia, New Zealand, India, Pakistan, Ceylon (now Sri Lanka) and South Africa – large parts of Africa such as Kenya, Rhodesia, (modern day Zimbabwe), Malawi and Zambia, Sierra Leone and the Gold Coast (now Ghana) were also pink on the map. Cyprus, Malta and Gibraltar represented the Mediterranean. There were also assorted islands around the world, from Fiji in the Pacific to Jamaica in the Caribbean to Tristan da Cunha in the South Atlantic. In Asia we had Malaya, Hong Kong and Singapore. I have probably forgotten a few.

We celebrated this mighty Empire every May on Empire Day. Conceived by Queen Victoria, the first Empire Day was celebrated a year after her death in May 1902. Empire Day would, in the words of the recently dead Queen *"Remind children that they formed part of the British Empire and that they might think with others in lands across the sea what it meant to be sons and daughters of such a glorious Empire. That the strength of the Empire depended on them and that they should never forget it"*

In truth though, the British Empire had already begun its long descent into dissolution by the end of the Second World War. Despite the fact that Britain in 1945 had been in reality a bankrupt nation after 6 years of hostilities, our leaders still did everything they could to try to bolster up our global Empire.

Even when in 1947 the US Congress had voted US$ 6 Billion under the Marshall Plan for the Regeneration of Europe, and individual countries had had to tender for a share of it.

Not everyone realises it, but Britain took the largest share (US$ 2.7 Billion - worth in today's money well over $ 50 Billion). The defeated Germans invested their share - of just US$ 1.7 Billion – mainly into building factories, and 60 years on are now the second largest exporter of Manufactured Goods in the world. Whereas British Governments of the 1950s squandered our share on delusions of Imperial Grandeur.

They continued to fund "Imperial strength" by keeping troops all over the colonies, even when it was clear to all that Britain was bust. To be able to do this the Attlee Government re-introduced compulsory National Service in 1947 for men only. For a term of 18 months. Later extended to 2 years. It was only finally abolished in 1960. The cost of this was crippling and ultimately futile. Thousands of brave British troops died for no result at all.

British Governments invested much of the remainder of the Marshall Plan funds into Gold Bullion in a vainglorious and also ultimately futile attempt to underpin the value of the Pound. This strengthened the delusion of successive Governments that they could support the continuation of the Sterling Area, and thereby maintain the Trading history of the Empire. This would prove to the World that Britannia still ruled the waves. That the Sun would never set on our glorious Empire.

It soon became apparent that this policy was a disaster. It represented probably the worst example of political hubris ever committed by an otherwise sane nation. (Although of course hindsight is a wonderful thing). The policy took a mortal blow however when the left wing Chancellor in the post war Labour

Government, Sir Stafford Cripps, devalued the pound by almost 50% against the US dollar in 1951. This had been viewed as a good thing as it made our exports more competitive. It would have been even better if only we had used some of the Marshall Plan funds for building the factories necessary to maximise those Exports in the first place!.

Although the British Monarch remained the Head of State of the Commonwealth countries, as well as Ruler of the above mentioned colonies, the tide of history was beginning to turn. Within 25 years most of them had gained independence – either with much blood letting and rearguard actions by we Brits, especially but not exclusively in Kenya and Cyprus - or with more peaceful transitions.

This had been due in part either to the arming of rebel groups by the Communists in Moscow, or through political pressure - and intervention - from power wielding American Presidents. The Suez crisis in 1956 being the most blatant example. What then of the "Special Relationship" our leaders still talk of today? Self delusion. To quote Lord Palmerston, Prime Minister in Victorian times, when Britannia truly did rule the waves "Nations do not have permanent allies; they have permanent interests" But this of course had been when we had had more gunboats than anyone else

*

The Empire had always had its darker side. Although at the time everyone in Britain either lived in genuine total ignorance of it - or just buried their heads in the sand. Because in the early 1950s the concept of racism simply did not exist in this sceptred isle. By today's standards we were all racists then - one way or another. The Crown and the Establishment continued to foster the propaganda that colonisation and British rule had been and was continuing to be of great benevolent benefit to the Monarch's "extended family" of brown black and yellow skinned subjects around the globe.

(As always there was some truth in this. We had left India with the largest railway network there has ever been, and gave them Democratic Government and a modern legal system. We had left behind us Westernised Democracies in Canada, Australia, New Zealand and a dozen other lands.) It was simply that there was no substitute for self determination. Even though in too many cases since self- rule has proved to be a signal failure.)

But we had also arbitrarily created whole new states in Africa and the Middle East across tribal and religious lines. So that when we left internecine tribal wars often broke out – and in places like the Sudan and Iraq still smoulder 50 years on.

This assertion of brotherhood however never for a moment ever extended to thinking of our "colonial brothers" - either here in Britain or even and often more especially in their own countries - as being our social or moral equals. The citizens of Canada, Australia, and New Zealand were perfectly acceptable as equals – but then of course they were all white skinned and mostly (then) of British stock. The Dutch Boers were white Europeans, but a Dutchman had once ruled us here in Britain so they were acceptable in "polite" company. Perhaps the thinking of the day is best summed up by the common expression of the pre - and - post war years of "play the white man old chap" made by one Englishman to another seeking fair play.

India had gained its Independence in 1947 but for the most part Indians themselves were largely considered inferior by most of us here in Britain - along with all the other black brown and yellow skinned members of this glorious global "family" My cousin George did in fact marry an Indian lady from Assam. Her name was Gladys (*yes really!*) and she was a very gracious and cultured lady. She had a seemingly endless wardrobe of brightly coloured saris. Their Anglo - Indian daughters were gorgeous. They and their brother Peter spent their childhoods largely in Private schools in the UK while George spent all his working life with Gladys in the colonies with Burma Oil. Life would have been much more problematic for them in the Britain of the 1950s. When they finally retired to Midhurst in the 1980s mixed race marriages raised far fewer eyebrows.

*

Wogs, Dagoes, Fuzzy Wuzzies, Chinks, Nig Nogs, Hindus, Pakis, Golliwogs – I am sorry, but these were just some of the derogatory terms that were in general use while I was growing up, and applied arbitrarily to any coloured member of this supposed glorious and blissful "extended family". If I say that I never used these racist words as a teenager in the late 50s and early 60s it would sadly be a lie. Maybe they would be restricted to jokes in the main - eg "a Paki and a Nig nog go into a pub —" but none the less pejorative for that.

Simply put, we we had all been brought up to believe that we Brits were simply somehow superior not just to the Dagoes in the colonies but to Dagoes everywhere. Turks, Eyeties - even Froggies. We had won the war hadn't we? Superiority and xenophobia ruled OK in our Island stronghold. We had a tacit social apartheid that was understood by all of us. We just took it for granted that we were somehow superior to coloureds and "natives".

It was into this still largely racist Britain of the early 1950s that the first immigrants were already disembarking off the banana boats from the islands of the Caribbean. Their arrival changed Britain forever. Britain had lost 500,000 men from its work force because of the war, and organisations like the NHS, London Transport and Metropolitan Councils across the nation were desperate to fill lower level jobs. Life was hard for this advance guard of what has since become our multi racial multi cultural society today – and not just in material terms. They and their descendants had to confront almost a subsequent half century of prejudice of the worst kind; viz. a hostile and largely racist Police force, Colin Jordan's British National Party, Enoch Powell and his rantings and ravings. Landlords who put signs outside their flats saying "No blacks" Golf clubs who would not let the wealthier of their number join as members. The list is almost endless.

Yet by the time of the National Census in the early 60s, over 175,000 residents put their place of birth as the West Indies. Today I guess at least 20 times that number would put their parents' birthplace as the same. Their arrival changed Britain forever

Holidays

We always looked forward to our summer holidays. For centuries the British man in the street had only ever crossed the Channel to Europe to fight wars of conquest. Hence the long list of pejorative names for European peoples set out overleaf. We in our island stronghold had always had a very dismissive view of Europe which we referred to universally as "The Continent". This was exemplified in the newspaper headline of the 1930s (possibly apocryphal) - "Fog in the Channel, Continent cut off" Only the very rich had ever ventured across the Channel, on The Grand Tour – creating some of the major French resorts such as Deauville, Biarritz, and Monte Carlo almost overnight. But this had been at its height in the 19th Century and up to 1930.

The Second World War had not only put that on hold, but Society had changed dramatically by 1945. In any case, in 1951 the man on the Clapham Omnibus had only recently returned from fighting yet another war on European soil, and would have no more thought of taking his nearest and dearest across the water than fly in the air. Which in the 1950's was also a rich man's pursuit. It would be another 20+ years before Air Holidays "took off" for the man in the street.

So we British went to the seaside. Our family went to Bognor Regis. The town had received the honorary "Regis" after its name from George V, who had convalesced there after an illness in the late 1920s. When on his death bed at Sandringham in 1936, he was told instead by an Equerry that he should soon be well enough to return to Bognor to convalesce in the town once again. It was then that he apparently uttered the now famed words "Bugger Bognor" They were not though, as often thought, to be his dying words. These were apparently unprintable.

We stayed in a Guest House just down from the beach huts at the Aldwick end of the town. As far as I can recall it was a B&B. I remember starched white tablecloths - and being personally served food at breakfast. One did feel grand. The first time we went was the very first time I had ever breathed the salty sea air. It is not something you ever forget. We rented a beach hut, brewed our own tea and Mum bought bread and ham and butter and made us all sandwiches.

We went to various cafés and tearooms in the town for other meals. I even recall that at one establishment we waited over an hour for our order before it was served by a young girl who was totally gormless. Why I should remember this after over 60 years I have no idea. Strange, but in the intervening period of years the British antipathy to personal service seems to have changed so little.

As an alternative to Restaurants, we would sometimes buy cod and chips from the local chip shop and eat it sitting on a bench in the Park that runs along behind the Promenade at Aldwick. Fish and chips wrapped in old newspapers were the only Fast

Food on sale in Britain in the early 1950s. Fish was freely available as it had never been rationed.

If I had to choose one single aroma that encapsulates the essence of the British seaside, indeed of the whole British way of life, it would have to be that of of Fish and chips smothered in salt and vinegar and wrapped in an old newspaper.

Another thing that I remember is that on the road back to our B&B there was an ice cream stand selling THE most exotic wares I had ever seen. Mint, Orange, Chocolate chip, Banana, and Tutti Frutti flavours were on sale alongside the more traditional Vanilla and Strawberry. You could have them in cones or in wafers (whatever happened to ice cream in wafers - you could get a better grip and thereby a larger mouthful holding a brick of ice cream horizontally rather than balancing a scoop of it on top of a cone). I did not wonder how the vendor had got so many flavours on sale in a time when food rationing was still in force – as I had never heard of food rationing then.

We went to Bognor for several years. Phil and I used to play tag behind the beach huts. We went shrimping at low tide in the rocks offshore, and did all those wonderful things that young children at the seaside do. However the real fun to be found in Bognor was at Hotham Park.

Opened in 1947, the year Phil was born, it had every family attraction you could wish for. My favourite – well I didn't have one to be honest. There were so many to choose from. There was the miniature railway that chugged around the grounds in clouds of steam, passing through tunnels made of corrugated iron and blowing its steam whistle. Then there was the boating lake with its small launches that had real petrol engines – only an adult was allowed to drive them. Although Dad, like most Dads, let me have a go steering and pushing the accelerator with my foot. The Park also had a putting green that gave Phil and I much entertainment. All in all Hotham Park was a fun place to be. I understand it is still open in reduced form. They seem to have kept the train!

There was one other holiday venue that I particularly remember as a child. One of our neighbours the Shilstones owned a chicken farm near Bexhill in Sussex. (One cannot even begin to speculate just how popular THEY must have been with post war rationing.!) So that year we went to Bexhill and were treated as guests at the farm. Have you ever screwed the head off a chicken while it is still alive? I have no idea whether this is even legal any longer. The chickens were all free range, and you would not believe how quickly a chicken can move across the ground if it sees you coming. The trick was to creep up on it, tighten both hands around its scrawny neck, then squeeze and twist violently in one movement. Believe me, it works a treat.

We also took two dozen eggs back home with us. *Shh, don't tell the Ministry of Food!!*

One year when I was about 9 we went to stay with my Aunt Dorothy in her bungalow in Kempston near Bedford. It always amused me to hear her calling Dad her "younger Brother". The most striking thing that I remember about her now was that she was the exact spitting image of the actress Joan Hickson who for many years played Miss Marple in the eponymous TV series. Like millions of spinster ladies of her generation, she had lost her true love in the trenches of the Somme in 1916. Men had been at a premium after the death toll of the Great War and she had never courted again. Dad told me she had also been in a road accident in the 1940s and had completely lost her sense of taste. Her drink of choice was warm water. Despite this she had still retained her sense of fun – running a Primary School probably helped.

Aunt Dorothy lived to over 90. There was one very poignant moment during her funeral in the late 1980s. As the coffin was being carried through the Lychgate on a cold snowy Winter's Day, the haunting sound of a barking dog fox could suddenly be clearly heard in the distance across the frozen fields. I like to think it was her lost love calling to her across the years. A good soul was Aunt Dorothy.

*

Horsepower

Being the core of a true "Garden Suburb" gardeners across the Knoll Estate would wait expectantly, bucket and spade in hand, for Joe Everest to appear. Joe was our milkman. He was tall athletic with fair hair. I imagine he might have set a few house-wives' hearts a flutter. But it was the horse that drew his cart that was of interest to the Gardening fraternity. They would follow the cart around the streets waiting for nature to take its course, then rush triumphantly back home and dig the results into the rose beds. It was Gardeners' heaven. Joe worked for Express Dairies – a bit of a misnomer I guess, as the poor horse managed maybe 5 mph. The neighbourhood kids like myself would sometimes be allowed to ride on the back of the cart. Boy did we feel important.

I do not know whether Joe captured the hearts of any ladies on his round. – but there was another milkman who apparently had. He too worked for Express Dairies. His name was Arthur, and he delivered at the top of Scads Hill. Where my best mate Graham lived. When he was 6 or 7 Graham used to help Arthur on his cart in the school holidays. Each morning as they approached a particular point on the round Arthur would get Graham to make the deliveries to a string of houses. While he sat on the cart on his own - with his hands in his pockets. Then Arthur would disappear into a house further down the road for 15 to 20 minutes while Graham watched the horse.

This happened most days. At the time Graham had had no idea what was going on. It was not until he reached puberty that he figured it out. While he was making deliveries for him Arthur would pleasure himself. Then just down the road he would pop in to visit his lady friend.

Benny Hill would have been proud.!!

Stanley Road slopes down appreciably so poor old dobbin must have found it hard to return up from the bottom. I have learnt recently from my old mate Colin, my schoolmate at St Nicholas in 1947 who traced me from Portugal a few years ago now, that the horse had had particular problems in winter. Lynwood Drive slopes sharply down at the Knoll Rise end. When the roads were icy the assembled neighbours had to push the cart back up the short sharp incline.

Horses formed a significant haulage solution after the war due to the continued rationing of petrol. As well as the milk, the Coalman delivered to local homes from a horse and cart as well. Coal was sold in multiples of a Hundredweight. 112 pounds weight. Our coal man – like I guess all coal men – was a big brawny chap. He needed to be as he had to haul half hundredweight sacks off the cart and then carry them on his back round to the back garden. and the coal bunker. Not entirely sure what he looked like as he spent his working days with his face covered in coal dust.

Phil and I were the only two young children in the road until the early 50s. Not too surprising as birth rates had been at an all time low during the war for obvious reasons. Most of the neighbours seemed to be quite a bit older than my parents. There were the Shilstones of course who lived two houses down on the opposite side of the road. They had two grown up children as I recall. The man who lived next door down to them was rather scrawny with a pencil moustache. He had a pale, sickly, somewhat haunted look about him. He kept himself very much to himself and did not socialise. I later learned that he had spent 4 years in a Japanese POW camp after the fall of Singapore.

The house opposite had a large secluded garden – you never saw much of them at all. They had a vicious little black Scottish Terrier that would bite your ankles as soon as look at you. Even Rover avoided him! Then of course there was the owner of the Commodore and his swimming pool at No 4. Next door there was a lady whose name was Mildred - who as far as I could make out was living with her aged Father. She was the one with the cat that terrorised Rover.

So it was great fun for me when Rover was about 4 years old and his arch nemesis the cat next door moved itself and it's Staff out, and the Shapiros moved in. I believe Mr Shapiro was a University lecturer They had two sons, one in his late teens, and David who was my age. I had never had a playmate living next door before. Stanley Road sloped down quite sharply, which made it an excellent place to run our toy cars. We each had a goodly collection of Dinky cars in their uniquely bright colours, together with vans and lorries. Pride of place in my collection was the red Maserati I had got for Christmas the previous year.

I also had a model of a white French *Saviem* coach (or "sharra-bang" from the French *char à bancs,* as everyone called them in those days) Being heavier and with a longer wheelbase you could push it further down the pavement than many a lighter vehicle. It was Formula One at weekends! The first time I ever stayed outside after dark without an adult present was on one of these marathon car racing sessions. It is just a pity that all my toy cars got lost or rusted away in the ensuing decades. Along with early editions of the comics I used to read, mint condition models of Dinky cars fetch hundreds, sometimes thousands at Auction today.

David became even more popular when I found out his Dad had installed a *Hornby* Train set in their loft. It had two main-lines, sidings, and a Pullman coach set pulled by a model of a Great Western King Class loco – the most beautiful engine ever built anywhere. I spent as much time as I could next door from then on. Mrs Shapiro used to bring us sandwiches for our lunch. I wonder what eventually became of the Shapiro family? They were the best neighbours a 10 year old boy could have wished for.

He and I paid regular visits every autumn to the huge spreading Horse Chestnut tree in Lucerne Road. Where we used to throw sticks up maybe 20-25 feet into the branches heavy with conkers. This activity often ended with us fleeing from the angry owner of the property, our pockets full with round shiny booty.

We used to soak the best conkers in vinegar, then bake them in the oven to make them harder before playing endlessly with them in the playground at school. I once had a 24er.

(*I understand now that ' Elf and Safety insist children wear goggles when playing conkers - in case bits fly off and get in your eye. Good job these politically correct idiots hadn't been around in the war – we would have had to surrender - as fighting would have been deemed to be too dangerous. God help future generations if this is social progress.*)

Phil had followed me to St Nicholas, and then started at Chislehurst Road Primary in the autumn of 1953. For 10 months I helped to shepherd him through his first full year, and walked with him to and from school. This turned out to be the only time we would ever spend at the same. school together.

PART TWO

A WHOLE NEW VISTA OPENS

||||||||||||||||||||||||||||||||||||||||||||||||||||||||||||||||

1954

1954 saw two events that changed the world. First, Roger Bannister became the first human being to run a sub four minute mile. Second, Bill Hayley and the Comets released their seminal work "Rock around the Clock" This had teenagers at their concerts rocking in the aisles, and most parents in America condemning the Group as being an "immoral influence" on the young. The song is now widely recognised as having brought Rock and Roll into mainstream music. Launching the career of Elvis a year later. The rest is history.

Then in August 1954 I passed the 11+, and graduated to Chislehurst and Sidcup Grammar School for Boys. (*There were no mixed sex schools in the 1950s. Boys went to one school and were taught by men, while girls went to Girls' schools and were taught by women. Saudi Arabians would have approved.*) On 9th September I caught the No 51 Bus from Orpington to Sidcup clad in my purple blazer and grey cap with the purple piping. As I soon learned, the middle button of the cap was cut off by older boys as some form of initiation ceremony. I walked with some trepidation down Hurst Road, doing my best to feign *sang froid* as I went, and set foot inside the architectural splendour that was Chis and Sid Grammar for the very first time.

What I did not know then was that so had everyone one else in the school that day, boys and Masters alike. Even the Headmaster was a new boy. The building had in fact only been completed several weeks before. How much do you think it might cost today to build a school to house 720 boys in 19 classrooms on two floors, together with specialist rooms for Science, a Dining suite, as well as a full size gym. £ 15 million? £20 million? Have a guess – the true figure will astound you. I will reveal it later in the book. So that you will be able to fully comprehend the corrosive effect of Inflation on our currency over the past 50+ years.

Chis and Sid had been founded in 1931. The School had been struggling to house a growing population ever since. The previous school premises, at Crittalls Corner in Sidcup, had been bombed in the Blitz. It had been patched up but under the new Educational Plan for the area set by the Tory Government Chis and Sid was given a larger catchment area, so it was decided to build the new school on the *Lamorbey* site in Hurst Road. There was room for 720 boys, with room for expansion further on the site, set as it was in 29 acres of open fields.

(In fact, with supreme irony another new school had also opened its doors just up the road in Kidbrooke in 1954. The first purpose built Comprehensive school in Britain.)

5 months after the school left the old premises for the last time, it's well loved Headmaster for the previous 20 years, Dr McGregor Williams, had died. I had gone to see him with Dad at the old school in August. All the new intake did. He seemed a kindly white haired old gent.

It soon became apparent that our new Headmaster, R R Pedley, merited none of those epithets. He had been 3 weeks away from his 42nd birthday when he took the helm at Chis and Sid in September 1954. He had been Head Boy at Sherborne before winning an Open Scholarship to Downing College Cambridge to read English. He served in the Royal Artillery during the war, leaving with the rank of Major. His previous position had been as Headmaster of the City Boys School in Leicester. He was a stocky and rather imposing chap, with a gruff voice. He was seldom if ever caught smiling. As we would all come to learn, he would turn up twice a term at your classroom to review the "marks sheets" kept by the masters on each boy, praise the successful, berate the unsuccessful and move on to the next.

He had always put particular emphasis on getting boys into the top Universities of Oxford and Cambridge. Whilst he was Headmaster and until he left in 1967 Chis and Sid placed more boys at Oxbridge than any other Grammar School in the land other than the much larger – and much more prestigious – Manchester Grammar School. Although many – including myself in hindsight – accuse him of concentrating too much on HIS arbitrarily chosen elite at the expense of the rest of the school. He was a driven man – and as such was pretty much universally hated by boys and staff alike.

The Grammar School rationale.

Looking back now, and in my opinion, the greatest sin ever perpetrated against British children by the State was the abolition of Grammar Schools. This was started by Shirley Williams in a Labour government in the 1970s – and then, quite unbelievably, finished off by that greatest proselytiser of self reliance and freedom of choice herself, Margaret Thatcher, in the 1980s. Yes, there have been fingers pointed at the process that got one there – the 11 plus exam itself. Nonetheless the simple truth is that the Grammar School system remains to this day the most open, democratic, egalitarian and aspirational form of free State Education ever devised to cater for bright children from all strata of society.

Yes, it followed that there would be more children from middle class homes amongst its pupil base – especially over 50 years ago - but that was due to nurture not nature. This was not the fault of Grammar Schools. On the other hand, my brother failed his 11+ and in 1958 went to Cray Valley Technical College, which was based in the same building – completely renovated - at Crittalls Corner that the School had vacated in 1954. So no middle class conspiracy there then. If you were good enough you got in. If you weren't you didn't. Class did not come in to it. There were several boys from Council Houses in my intake that I know of. I am sure there were more.

In 1954 Grammar Schools were – rightly – considered to be centres of Excellence. It is reckoned that the top tier of 6 – 8 % of children academically went up to Grammar School in 1954. Of these, only maybe 50% - 60% even went on to do A levels, let alone go to Uni. At best maybe only 3/4 % of total children for any given year got there. Do the Maths. A tiny proportion.

This is the difference in value between Academic Excellence in the 1950s and today. Present day standards in Education have in fact sunk so low, that today the Confederation of British Industry constantly complains that their members cannot find sufficient applicants with the necessary numeracy and literacy skills to fulfil even basic job requirements. Oxford and Cambridge now set their own post A level Entry examinations for applicants even with good A levels. As they consider these to have become so devalued. This is why I and all Grammar school pupils of my era – of both sexes - as well as those fortunate to attend the remaining Grammars today – feel duly privileged. Excellence is a state of mind.

This view is of course far from being *"au courant"* these days. Equality for all in Education was the battle cry of the Labour Governments of Tony Blair (*educated privately at Fettes, the leading independent school in Scotland: fees 2013, £7, 300 per term*).

I can only quote the observation of W S Gilbert - "When every-one is somebody, nobody is anybody".

*

On my first day at Chis and Sid in 1954 I knew none of this. We new boys in our purple blazers were ushered into the Hall for our first Assembly. The whole school was there. New boys sat right at the back as I recall. The Headmaster and some senior members of his staff stood on the stage in their black gowns. They looked vaguely menacing, like vultures waiting to feast on their prey. Hymns were sung, prayers were said, and then R R Pedley made various announcements about school events. I felt more than a little overawed by it all.

(Mr Nigel Walker, the present Headmaster of Chis and Sid, which I am delighted to report very much still exists, has recently been kind enough to send me my School Record Card from the archive. This covers my entire time at the school Term by Term over the full 7 years I was there). This shows that I spent the first year in Form 2c. As I recall this was on the first floor. The Autumn term of 1954 went past largely in a blur of initiation.

Class timetables were handed out, English, Maths, French, Latin, History, Geography, Biology Chemistry Physics and RE. Masters introduced themselves and entered our names into their Class Registers. Maths sets and compasses, pencil boxes containing H, HB and B pencils, erasers, rulers, pencil sharpen-ers, bottles of ink to fill our ink wells and writing pens with fresh nibs were all placed into the drawers of desks which already had the names of several of their previous users carved into them. Gym kit was checked, text books for all subjects were issued (some dog eared, some new) - enough to equip a small library or so it seemed - and the daily educative round began.

The next thing you had to learn was the layout of this large sprawling school building. The Biology and Chemistry labs, the Masters Common Room, the Headmaster's study – so that you could walk silently by it – and the Gym. Which was my least favourite place. It was not as though I was unfit – after all, I had just come through 11 years of rationing, and had been walking absolutely everywhere since the age of 2. With an immune system that had got me through measles epidemics, polio, diptheria and the other terrible childhood diseases of my age. I was fine thanks.

This was not how my arch nemesis, the school's newly appointed Welsh PE Master and borderline sadist Milton "Bert" Williams, saw it. In 1954 nearly all school Masters in their mid thirties would have seen service in the war. He had served in the Royal Navy, had been an international gymnast and a boxing coach. He also had this pretentious habit of stalking around everywhere on the tips of his training shoes, as if somehow to emphasise just how super fit he was. In seven years I never saw him out of a tracksuit, even on the stage at Assembly.

We developed a healthy contempt for each other from Day One. It is crystal clear now, looking back, that the main purpose of such physical jerks for boys at that time in our history had been to prepare us for battle. Where else in life would we expect to roll forward across a floor or climb ropes for heavens sake? How many times has anyone reading this ever been OBLIGED to do such things in the real world? (Unless you are or once were in the Armed Forces, the Fire Service or the Coastguard.) PE became a weekly penance for me – vaulting over horses, trying to stand on my head (why for God's sake – did it improve scholastic ability?) - and failing miserably to complete a forward roll. I freely admit it – I had a morbid dread of breaking my neck. As the weeks months and years rolled by (*sorry about that*) it became a war of attrition between me and Milton.

The other important port of call was the Dining Hall. We had a morning break when free milk was distributed in the Hall in half pint bottles – considered an important element in child nutrition for the calcium it put into our bones. You could also buy doughnuts! We had a two sitting lunch system. The food was very much like the food you got everywhere else in 1954 – plain, not really filling, and bland. When we had stew (every other day it seemed) the pepper pots on the tables came in very handy to give some flavour – any flavour – to the meat and gravy. The one dish that I recall I really enjoyed for its culinary nature was Gypsy Tart for pudding.

The Masters were definitely an eccentric bunch. My favourite was John Walsh, Head of English. He hated Pedley with a loathing that was almost palpable – which endeared him greatly to the boys he taught. You could sometimes hear him from halfway down the ground floor corridor shouting at Pedley in his study at the far end. by the Main staircase. What was far less endearing for the boys about Walshie was his unerring ability to take out any boy in the classroom at will, sometimes without even looking up from his desk, with a wooden backed Blackboard duster at the first attempt – bloody hell it hurt!

At other times he would come into the classroom and without saying a word draw a picture of a fat woman in a tu tu ballet skirt on the blackboard. He called her his *"large scale Czechova"* - which meant naturally that it was time to revise. One of life's true eccentrics and well liked by everyone as I remember.

He was not alone in being a tad eccentric. For example, there was Mr Daniel Grindrod the Geography Master. You knew him instantly by his bald multi coloured head, a patchwork of red orange and brown splotches. His sight was not very good, and whenever there was some sniggering or other at the back of the room he would utter those immortal words that have followed all those he taught down the years - *"I can hear a boy grinning"*. We later learned that he had no hair as it had been burned off in a submarine fire during the war and the patchy nature of his scalp colour was early plastic surgery. A brave submariner.

Then there was Mr "Taffy" Jenkins. He taught French and spoke it with a fairly broad Carmarthen accent. When a boy once asked him what "Romantic" meant as in "a Romantic poet", he gave the byzantine and impenetrable reply "**Romantic is like what happens in a novel**". So that's clear enough then: a Romantic novel is —?

His favourite story was when he went on a school trip as a young man to pre war Germany in the Thirties. Apparently, when the pupils of the host school stood up at their assemblies, gave the Nazi salute and shouted "Heil Hitler" the Welsh group would join in – doubtless under instructions from Neville Chamberlain. Several of the boys in his group had devised an alternative. When the Germans and some of the Welsh shouted "*Heil Hitler*" they would shout "*Drei liter*" - three litres. As a German speaker I can tell you it works well if shouted loudly and quickly enough.

Another eccentric was "Nobby" Clarke the History Master. He was a quietly spoken chap most of the time. Sometimes though, midway through a lesson, he would suddenly stop in mid sentence and a blank look would come over his face. We all knew what was coming next. He would jump up from his desk and rush towards the back of the classroom, moustache bristling, gesticulating passionately at some invisible protagonist whilst making some key point known only to him about Napoleon and the like. The story going around the school was that he had got too much sun when fighting with the 8th Army in the Desert and it had turned his mind a little. He was a bit barmy, but harmless, and quite a good teacher apart from his little eccentricities.

Another source of much merriment amongst 2c was Mr Abthorp, the French Master we had in the first year He was universally known as the Mekon. Painted green and sat on a tea tray he would have been able to play the role of Dan Dare's arch enemy without make up or prosthetics. Yet I do recall that in one set of lessons he gave us perhaps THE most valuable insight into speaking French that I have ever experienced since. Exactly the right way to pronounce the vowel groups and diphthongs that infest the French language. Especially the five different ways you could pronounce the letter "e". That and how to speak through the nose. Anyone who speaks French will understand. It was just a pity he had not sat down with Taffy Jenkins for a few hours!

Corporal punishment

A common factor amongst almost all the Masters was a seeming predilection for Corporal punishment. Pedley had the cane, a swishy piece of bamboo that hurt like hell across the palms of the hand. Walshie was a dead shot with a board duster. Other Masters had their weapon of personal choice. Then there was L C Pascoe, Head of Maths and terror of the lunch hall. He had the habit of seizing the collars of misbehaving boys and dragging them by their necks up and out from the bench they were sitting on. This went on all the time - until on one occasion one victim, Trevor Oxley, turned blue and fainted. LCP would be banged up for that today for sure. Rightly.

Being whacked a few times at school for some misdemeanour or another does not seem to have had any lasting effect on my life. Indeed until I began this book I had not given it a thought in 50 odd years. It is certainly true that many teachers in my time could be too ready to lash out, and punishment of any kind should never be arbitrary or indiscriminate. But our teachers then were not sadists – with maybe the exception of Milton Williams. They did not cane you or throw board dusters at you for enjoyment – they did it to contain and control where necessary.

We certainly never beat our own kids when they were young. Equally we did smack their legs, or give them a poke with our fingers or forcibly grab them by the arms when they were having a paddy - or if they were trying to immolate themselves under the wheels of a passing car. All that was hurt was their pride. We did it for their own good.

Today this could get us arrested. So surely today the pendulum has swung far too far the other way. Why should responsible parents be answerable to the State for actions taken in the best interests of their offspring?. If you ASSAULT a child then you should be locked up. If you discipline a child fairly with a smack on the leg you should be applauded. Any society that cannot differentiate between the two is being run by extremely stupid people.

It is even worse in our schools today. My wife was a Primary teacher for 40 years. She took early retirement in 2005 to nurse her Mother for 3 years before she died. When she started her career Teachers were able to restrain and control children if they misbehaved, put plasters on their cuts, give them their medicines if they needed them, sanction them if they would not be quiet, shout at them if necessary. Now thanks to mindless politically correct Busybodies and Do-Gooders a teacher can no longer TOUCH a child in any way at all, not even to ASSIST them. They are also no longer allowed to shout at them or sanction their behaviour in any way at all that might be accusatory - in case they hurt their poor charges' feelings!!!

The results are all around us in Society today. The undisciplined Second Generation rowdy offspring of First Generation undisciplined and anti- social parents, neither of whom have any respect for authority (for they have never known discipline or authority, nor ever been subjected to or taught it). Who bad mouth anyone who dares to question their outrageous behaviour, secure in the knowledge that they have the law, Social workers and their "'Uman Rights" on their side. (*"'uman responsibilities – what are they then?"*)

Political correctness WILL destroy us all if the "Do Gooders" are not contained. The rule of Nanny must be curbed. Along with little – and big - monsters.

*

Being 1954 many of the Masters smoked like chimneys. There may have been a day that Cedric Morley, Physics Master, could not be found smoking at the back of one of his lessons, but nobody could remember when that might have been. Political correctness – what was that?

My first term passed largely uneventfully. The workload was heavy – two hours homework a night minimum across 7 subjects. The catchment area of the school was quite large. There were boys in my class from Green Street Green, on the A21 to Sevenoaks south of Orpington, to Eltham in South London to the North. Much of the main catchment area – Chislehurst, Petts Wood, Orpington and the Crays – had high levels of middle and professional class families. Most of us had a minimum 30+ minutes journey each way.

As a result it was not really possible to see school chums at the weekends as the travel options then were limited to just one – the bus. Roger Hardiman lived in Eltham as I remember and Denis Oliver lived out that way too. At the age of 12 we didn't get much in the way of pocket money.

I was slowly getting to know some of the Orpington boys – Roger Wild and Will Smith to name but two. My old mate

Colin was of course from my neighbourhood. Another local boy with whom I also later became close mates was Johnny Baker, with whom I met up again three years ago after almost 50 years, and to whom I owe a great debt for his invaluable input to this book.

2c had 31 boys. I know for a fact from subsequent research that at least 6 of them were Council house kids. Maybe there were more. In 1954 this meant coming from seriously disadvantaged family backgrounds. (There again, none of us had very much - and they would have had much less than that)

My report card shows that I was in the middle range of achievement. 21st in Term 1, 13th in Term 2, 23rd in Term 3. This proved quite conclusively that I was not a genius. This was a relief to all except my parents.

1955

The Winter of 1955 was a brutal one. The coldest for nearly a decade. Snowdrifts of up to 30 feet deep were recorded in the Highlands of Scotland. The RAF had to make emergency air drops of food and medicines to communities that remained cut off for weeks. Our school – all schools in the area – stayed open regardless. The 51 buses went on running despite the weather. There were far fewer obstacles in their way as the traffic levels then were less than 10% of what they are now. So it was practically a matter of honour to get in.

No wusses us - we all had stout shoes, scarves and overcoats didn't we? A little snow was not going to disrupt our education. Some of us might slip on the ice and land on our backsides, or twist an ankle, but hey – this was a small price to pay for being a Grammar School boy. (The pavements down Hurst Road soon became about as dangerous as the Cresta Run as 700 boys practised their sliding manoeuvres. The residents must have cursed us.) Our parents were of the same do or die mind. After all only 10 years before the majority of our Fathers had been fighting the Hun – a few bruises were nothing.

Once in school we pupils of Chis and Sid had a grand time in the lunch hour. There were loosely organised snowball battles on the field. The sight of groups of some 100 or so boys on each side throwing thousands of snowballs at each other was almost balletic – a winter wonderland with attitude!

On 16th January an even worse weather phenomenon struck the South East. Residents in London suddenly experienced what they thought must be an unheralded total eclipse of the sun. The sky turned totally and impenetrably dark at 1.15 in the afternoon. With memories of the Blitz still implanted in their minds, it is recorded that there was semi panic. Thousands of calls were made to 999, flooding the system. Some even thought the end of the World was nigh. The cause of the darkness was something equally sinister – freak wind conditions had collected all the considerable pollution over the London area and moulded it into a cloud layer of filth estimated to be 1 Kilometre thick. A combination of the smoke from fossil fuel burning and exhaust fumes from the growing number of internal combustion engines on the streets came back to haunt and poison the populace that day.

Smog had been an everyday winter occurrence in London for many years. The last Great Smog had been three years before. Over 400 people had died as a direct result. They say you could not see your hand in front of your face for days – many just fell into the Thames and drowned. After it cleared the Government began to consider action. But this "blackout" had been the last straw. The Clean Air Act came into force a few years later.

1955 was a momentous year across the Globe.

In April Albert Einstein died in the US State of New Jersey aged 76.

Churchill finally relinquished the reins of power due largely to old age and Anthony Eden became Prime Minister.

West Germany became a sovereign state under its first Chancellor Konrad Adenauer -

— and Rosa Parks refused to sit at the back of the bus in Montgomery Alabama. This resulted in Martin Luther King leading a year long boycott of the Montgomery Bus Co. Finally in 1956, the first de-segregated bus service in the South took to the streets. The Civil Rights movement was born.

"On the Waterfront" starring Marlon Brando won best picture at the Oscars in 1955. Any film with Marlon Brando AND Rod Steiger was bound to win. Brando won best Actor. But the film only came 6th in the money list. "Rear Window" the Hitchcock film starring James Stewart and Grace Kelly grossed over three times as much, followed by "20,000 leagues under the Sea" with Kirk Douglas and James Mason and "The Caine Mutiny" with Humphrey Bogart and Fred Mc Murray. James Dean's star went super nova with "Rebel without a Cause" and "East of Eden" - then on September the 30th flared and died. Aged just 24, he totalled his Porsche against a telegraph pole. DOA.

1955 was also the year that Emmanuel stopped growing. In September the previous year Emmanuel had been one of the biggest and tallest boys in our new intake. He had taken full advantage of this by terrorising the smaller boys and generally thugging his way around our year. But 9 months is a long time in the growth cycle of 12 year old boys. By June 1955 a lot of us had overtaken Emmanuel in size. By the end of the year Emmanuel was one of the smaller boys amongst his contemporaries. I would imagine that he did not enjoy his second year at Chis and Sid.

In May the Headmaster announced that the school would hold a Mock Election to mirror the actual General Election taking place on May 26th. Step forward Peter Birks. Recently arrived at the school from a Tea Plantation in India, he was one or two years ahead of me – cannot recall exactly. Big for his age, he was also a larger than life character who quickly made his presence felt. He rapidly gathered a cabal of some of the more eccentric boys around him.

Excited by Election fever, he decided to stand as a candidate in the Mock Election - for the Fascist Party. He won hands down – largely because he gave out free doughnuts with every vote. (*Yes I voted for him!*) Pedley was more than a little peeved – which Birks later told people had largely been the point. Nobody at the school ever liked Pedley.

Despite Pedley's displeasure, Birks became one of his blue eyed boys and went on to become Regius Professor of Civil Law at Oxford University. He died in 2003 at the age of 62.

*

The Spring of 1955 also saw the demise of football at the school after another team, Roan, had thumped the school team 12 – 1. From the autumn term Rugby became the official winter game. This disappointed many people, and apparently even Pedley, who had been a football player himself, expressed mis-givings at its demise. But he was bolstered by the thought that Rugby was played at Public schools. So in his mind it was only appropriate.

For me sport was more a summer thing. I enjoyed tennis. I was a passable off spin bowler – but in no way good enough to play for the School. That year John Flower took 78 wickets for the First X1 in a season – a record which I understand has never been equalled to this day.

(*In fact my best ever bowling figures were achieved in 1979, playing against the MCC. I shall never forget them: 3 overs, 2 maidens, 3 wickets for 2 runs. Do not reach for your copy of Wisden. It was in the Puerto de Hierro in Madrid, playing for the Ex-Pats against the eponymous Madrid Cricket Club.*)

*

By 1955 the economy was starting to accelerate after a decade of rationing. House building was roaring ahead. More houses would end up being built in the 1950s than in any decade before - or since. However, although petrol rationing had technically been abolished in 1950, this had had little effect on traffic numbers. Many cars had rusted away from a decade of non use, and all large cars had been confiscated at the beginning of the war and turned into ambulances and vans

Wheels

So it was not until the beginning of 1955 that Dad had purchased our first car – a second hand Morris 10. Apart from having four wheels, four seats and an engine, cars of that era bore little resemblance to a modern car. It had an 1140cc engine producing 37 brake horsepower; 0 – 50 mph took TWENTY THREE SECONDS. With a top speed of 60mph. Although this was definitely not to be recommended. It came with a set of travel blankets in the boot – the only way to keep warm in winter as there was no heater. There was no radio. Seat belts had still not been heard of.

The last of this particular model had rolled off the production line in 1948, which meant that the technology used was pre war. It was not a great car in which to be a back seat passenger. It wallowed a bit round bends if you took them at over 25 – 30 mph. Every time we went out for a drive there was a strong whiff of exhaust fumes that often led to nausea and travel sickness. The engine overheated quickly going up hill. It had also tried to get me killed!

The primitive suspension had been to blame. While we were wallowing in customary fashion round a bend on the road from Petts Wood to Chislehurst one Sunday the nearside back door suddenly flew open – and I flew out! How on Earth did I manage that you might ask? It was because the rear doors on

Morris cars from that era opened BACKWARDS. So as soon as the door flew open the whole width of the door frame was exposed - plenty enough room for the boy to shoot through. Happily there were grass verges alongside most of the roads in that area, so I had a soft landing.

I remember on our summer holidays that year we went to Lynton in North Devon. The town had been overwhelmed by floods in 1952, and there had been many deaths. We had to wait half an hour halfway up Porlock Hill on the A39 in North Devon (a 1: 4 gradient) for the radiator to stop steaming. Not only the suspension but also the steering were rudimentary by modern standards. We loved it – despite the travel sickness. There were still only 200,000 private cars registered in the UK in 1955, so driving was still a pleasure.

It was on this same summer holiday that we took a trip to Blackpool Sands, an idyllic spot on the South Devon Coast. The sands were almost white and pristine. The sea was the clearest I had ever seen it before - or since. Just beyond the shoreline there were dark rocks, giving it a black hue. Hence the name. We spent several hours there. I lingered too long in the sun and contracted sunstroke. Essentially this is the opposite to hypothermia – hyperthermia. Too much sun on the head and neck makes the body overheat. You get a high fever and nausea. Very unpleasant-I vowed to take more care not to sunbathe for too long. Another of life's lessons learnt.

On a long journey Dad had to try to plot a route that had petrol stations along it. This is why every 15-20 miles or so on a main road (almost exclusively single lane carriageways in each direction) you came across a yellow and black painted AA Box, often with a smartly uniformed peak capped AA man astride his motorbike and side. He smartly saluted you if there was an AA Members' badge on the radiator.

When you did find a petrol station you did not have to leave the car. The attendant filled the car for you, checked the oil if required, washed the windscreen where necessary, took your money, brought back any change and wished you a pleasant journey. Self service lay a long time in to the future.

Yes, motoring then was still a relaxation and a pleasure...

*

In September 1955 I was promoted to 3b. This year was to be my least successful of the 7. In the third semester I actually managed last out of 28. There was no real reason for this – maybe it was just hormonal. I do not think that it was the arrival of Mr "Mugsy" Mayatt for Maths to replace Mr Eyles. Whereas he had been a very experienced teacher of long service with great patience, and blessed with an almost avuncular nature, "Mugsy" was much younger (could even have been his first job) highly neurotic and swift to criticise. He had no empathy. He proved to be the final nail in the coffin of my desperate attempt to master the mysteries of Algebra. And Trigonometry. As I was stuck with him for the next three years.

As a 12 year old in the mid 1950s, not much else of consequence happened that year.

1956

||||||||||||||||||||||||||||||||||||||||||||||||||||||||||||||||

The Suez Crisis

1956 effectively marked the end of Britain as a World Power. Earlier in the year, Britain and the US had withdrawn an offer to finance the building of the Aswan Dam in Egypt due to the fact that the new leader of the country Colonel Nasser, who had recently deposed King Farouk in a military coup, had signed a new co-operation agreement with the Soviet Union. Prior to that he had already recognised the People's Republic of China in its struggles with Taiwan.

In retaliation for this, on 26th July 1956, President Nasser nationalised the Suez Canal. This caused panic in Whitehall, as the canal was a vital asset to Britain and represented a short-cut from Britain to India, and to her colonies and dominions in Asia and to Australia. The Trade of the Empire was genuinely imperilled.

Israel saw this as an act of aggression and as an opportunity to invade Egypt - and took it. Two days later the British and French Governments sided with them, and began to bomb Cairo. British paratroops were dropped in Sinai, and within a few days, in alliance with Jerusalem, the Canal Zone had been retaken. The Israelis had also secured most of their military objective, which had been to establish a permanent "cordon sanitaire" on the border with Egypt. Then came the bombshell – the American Government refused to sanction the British action at the UN.

Despite the fact that Nasser was a Communist sympathiser, and that 1956 was the height of the Cold War, as well as the fact that they had always supported the State of Israel, the US brought pressure on the three allies, through their power of veto on the Security Council, to cease their military actions and withdraw. The British Government caved in and did so. One immediate result of this was the re-introduction of petrol rationing until late the following year.

The US justified their decision publicly as a protest against further "gunboat diplomacy" in a post colonial world. There is no doubt at all in most observers' minds however that the US had seen the Suez crisis as a way to mortally wound the British Empire: as a decisive nail in the coffin of the Free Trade area between Britain and its Commonwealth partners. The US had always been bitterly opposed to these Commonwealth Preferential Tariffs. Not too surprisingly, as they had been set up in the early 1930s precisely to combat the tariff barriers set up by Washington to protect. their own Import Tariffs. As always, it came down to business in the end.

Our new school building was officially opened by a bevy of dignitaries on the 11th of May 1956. Just as well, for about the same time the Shadow Labour Education Secretary Anthony Crosland (privately educated at Highgate School) published his treatise "The Future of Socialism" that demanded an "egalitarian Comprehensive means of teaching" and swore death and destruction on Grammar Schools. However he would have to wait another 8 years before beginning to implement his policy in a Labour Government. Just as well for me.

Discipline and the Dress code were essential parts of Grammar School life in the 1950s. The uniform identified you as a member of an elite. Woe betide the boy spotted without his cap on his head on the walk to and from school. Or on hot days, with his purple blazer scrunched into his satchel or slung over his shoulder. You were not just letting yourself down, you were letting the school down. Detention was the mildest form of punishment for infringements of the Dress Code. My good mate John Baker tells me that on one end of Summer term, as he was leaving the building, my nemesis Milton saw him without a cap and sent him to stand outside Pedley's study.

In the outside world at that time things were rather different for many teenagers. The Teddy boy was in the ascendancy. They got their name from the Edwardian style of clothes that they wore. This was almost ritualistic – severely tapered trousers with long jackets and brightly coloured waistcoats. Always tailor made and paid for on tick. On their feet they wore either Cuban heeled zip up boots known as winkle pickers or thick rubber - soled suede shoes known as brothel creepers. They all thought that they were the bees knees. Typically they hung around in large groups, especially outside the many Dance Halls of the day, chatting up the girls and running combs endlessly through their hair-oil-soaked, swept back rockabilly quiff tonsures. But when in 1956 the Hollywood film "The Blackboard Jungle" was shown at the Elephant and Castle in South London – the spiritual home of the Ted – the largely Teddy boy audience rioted, tore up the seats and danced in the aisles. There were Ted riots at every subsequent showing of the film in the UK

What had started as a dress code was turning uglier by the day. Pitched battles between rival Teddy Boy gangs erupted in City streets across Britain (especially in London). The favourite weapon was the flick knife. One Ted said on TV this was because when folded up it did not disturb the line of the jacket. (Early Teds had also been known as "Cosh boys", with special cosh pockets sewn into their tailored jackets.) Teds were around for some 20 years, but had morphed back into a gentler life style by the mid 60s. They had been the vanguard for the rebellious youth of the Swinging Sixties that followed them. Influenced their dress design.

In September I advanced to 4B. I did better in 4B than I had in 3B (when you are at the bottom, the only way is up!!) We also had a new Biology teacher that year, "Doc" King. I remember even now that he was the smartest dressed teacher I had ever come across (and not JUST because that would not have been hard to achieve given the general sartorial standard of the Staff Room – where beige cardigans and green corduroy trousers reigned supreme). He always wore a smart well cut dark suit, collar and tie. I remember that before each lesson he would impress upon us that we were the "cream" - both to encourage us in our education and doubtless to echo Pedley's mantra.

Through the grapevine that flourishes in every school, and even though you can never remember when you heard it first, his nickname of "Doc" was well founded. He had spent a number of years at Medical School, with his heart set on becoming a surgeon. However he eventually discovered that he possessed a quality unsuited for surgery – he could not stand the sight of blood, and fainted clean away in the Theatre at the sight of it. A bit awkward that.

*

1956 was also a year for other momentous events globally.

In February the Soviet Premier Nikita Kruschev publicly denounced the "excesses" of Stalin. This gave the world hope that the Soviet Union might be moving towards to some form of *détente* with the West This hope was soon dashed. Foolishly believing that Moscow would not intervene after Kruschev's speech, on 23rd October there was a populist uprising by the Hungarians against their Government and its Soviet policies. In the ensuing battles between rapidly formed People's Militias and the State Security Police and locally based Soviet troops over 2,500 citizens and 700 troops and police were killed.

17 days later, after first agreeing to talks, Moscow then reneged and sent in the tanks to restore order. Ringleaders were shot or disappeared. Thousands of refugees crossed the Austrian border. The suppression of Hungary disenchanted many Marxists in the West – but Moscow cemented its power over Eastern Europe for another 33 years. So much for Stalin.

*

1956 also saw another revolution – this time in pop music in the West. Following the runaway success of Bill Haley and the Comets, a new colossus appeared on the scene. Someone who even to this day is considered the Greatest, with tens of thousands of impersonators – yes, it was Elvis. His two record releases that year - "Hound Dog" and "Heartbreak Hotel" have since sold countless millions of copies - and are still selling today almost 60 years on. He also made the first of several blockbuster movies this year - "Love me Tender". The world of pop would never be the same again.

(One particular sporting feat of 1956 also warrants a special mention. In June 1956, at the 2nd Test Match against Australia at Old Trafford the Surrey and England spin bowler Jim Laker took all 10 wickets in the First Innings - and 9 wickets in the 2nd - for a final total of 19 – 90. No bowler in a Test Match has ever equalled this to this day.)

Meanwhile in Hollywood "Around the World" in 80 Days with David Niven won best Film at the Oscars. (Although "The Ten Commandments" with Charlton Heston grossed twice as much at the Box office. Was this because of the religious overtones of the latter, or because the former included references to foreign parts of the Globe alien to most people – and especially to Americans?). "The King and I" with Yul Brynner and Deborah Kerr and "Giant" with Rock Hudson were also honourable contenders.

While all of this was happening in the world outside, School life rolled inexorably on. Towards the end of the summer a Jubilee Ball had been held for the 6th form to celebrate the fact that only 4 other schools had sent more boys to Oxbridge than Chis and Sid. End of term saw the Jubilee Fete which raised £500 for the Sports Pavilion (a lot of money in 1956). Then it was back to the seaside for the Proom family – this time to Swanage.

Swanage was a quiet place. As an outside observer today it seems to me to have vanished off the map. I do not believe that I have heard any mention of the place from any source since that time. I loved Studland Bay nearby, where the tide went out so far Phil and I could walk miles out to sea, or just paddle endlessly looking for rock pools and use our shrimping nets to catch crabs - and sometimes a star fish! One day we stayed in the sun too long and turned a violent shade of red. Then had to spend a couple of days swathed in calamine lotion. Would I never learn? For the second year in a row my sun worshipping had gone far too far.

One other great pleasure of seaside holidays was kite flying. Every boy had a kite in those days, and the sky above the shoreline was dotted with streamers of every colour of the rainbow as the kites dipped and weaved and soared in tune with the wind. There is one kite I had that was very special. Rather than having a sail to catch the wind, this one was an aeroplane whose wings rotated to give it lift. In a strong wind they made a rattling sound a bit like machine gun noise as it soared into the breeze. I spent a long time looking for something similar when our kids came along, but never could find one.

One thing I remember liking about the area on the Isle of Purbeck where Swanage sits were some of the place names. One in particular has always stuck in my mind – why does the memory retain over decades one nugget of trivia over others it discards?

I have no recollection where exactly we stayed in Swanage – I just know it was a Guest House - but I remember quite clearly Studland Bay, and the name of a local village – Langton Matravers. The name conjures up visions of a a Matinee Idol - "Langton Matravers in Blithe Spirit at the Adelphi". Remarkable thing memory.

Green fingers

Gardening was part of our life in the 50s. One of the first things we did after we got back from holiday each year was to see how far the runner beans had climbed up the small forest of poles in the bottom half of the garden. Were the green shoots now covered in the red flowers that meant green beans were on the way? In a garden the size of ours there was always much work to be done. From as early as I could remember I had helped Dad. On one occasion – I think I was about 4 - I was assigned a flower bed, on the right hand side of the garden next to the bullace tree where I could plant as I pleased. I can assure you that there is no greater satisfaction when you are 4 years old than to plant a peony, and see it sprout up and produce that uniquely textured deep red ball of petals.

Another time I remember was when I was about 6. I was digging with my trowel under one of the 11 apple trees on the other side of the garden when I found a threepenny bit. I went on digging and unearthed other coins including a sixpence. I ran inside the house and excitedly showed them to Mum. Then went back and unearthed more treasure trove. Dad had been working in the garden at the time, so I remained – and remain to this day – unsure whether the coins had been planted by him, or whether they really had been left there by a previous owner.

The apple trees ran down the left hand side of the garden behind the flower beds, Behind them ran a pathway alongside the privet hedge. One of the most satisfying things for me about gardening was to cut and trim this hedge - with manual shears. It took more than a little while. It was not enough for me – Mr Fussy – to cut the hedge. It had to be even. This is what took the time. No barber could have got those hedges straighter. I like to think we had the smartest hedges in the area. On the other hand the lime tree in the front garden, grown horizontally like a wisteria above the fence, needed to be pruned with secateurs every autumn. Out came the steps, on to the pavement, up went the boy – snip snip. Another couple of hours passed by.

The lawn mower was of course a push me pull you, so you could only cut the grass on a dry day. It was fatal to let the grass grow too long, in which event you had to cut it with a scythe as the small barrel of the mower just gave up the ghost. Gardening remained hard and satisfying work before Messrs Black and Decker came on the scene. I loved every second of it – rural pastimes in a suburban setting. That is what the Knoll Estate was all about.

In the Summer Term the Debating Society proposed the motion "The Goon Show is insulting to the public's intelligence" Bloody sacrilege! It was predictably heavily defeated – after which I spent another Tuesday evening under the blankets with my cat's whisker listening to the plangent tone of Eccles reciting "He's fallen in the water" and Neddy Seagoon uttering the immortal phrase "Have a gorilla". Over and over again. Bliss.

*

It was during the Summer holidays that Alan Smith and I invented hand tennis – or maybe you could have called it horizontal *pelota*. The Rules were simple – first, you marked out a playing area on the grass with whatever came to hand. (We had a good stock of long beanpoles that we used to outline the Court and mark a halfway line) You can play singles or doubles. Players must remain kneeling at all times. You play with a normal tennis ball and bat it back and forward with just the palm of your hand. Arm or fist is a foul shot. The same rules as tennis apply. A ball is in or out. It must not bounce twice. It sounds mundane, but believe me things can get pretty hectic – you try returning a fast ball out of immediate reach whilst remaining on your knees! It involves gymnastic agility. So in case someone else should invent such a sport, unlikely as that may be – although after synchronised swimming frankly anything is possible – I will tell them where to send the Royalty cheques.

1957

At the beginning of 1957 I recall that there was much hoohah at one morning Assembly at which the portrait of the late Dr McGregor Williams, the previous Headmaster, had been unveiled. There was general agreement that Dr Williams had been a much loved and sympathetic leader of the school – accusations that could never have been levelled at R R Pedley Esq.

The School Orchestra gave a recital. If there is one thing I regret it is that I never learnt to play a musical instrument. I had had basic piano lessons from the nice lady teacher in her front room round the corner in Keswick Road, and had learned the maxim "Every Good Boy Deserves Fruit". I had practised my basic scales – but that was about it. In the summer term the School's first full time Music Master Steve Dunball would be appointed, replacing the part time Music and Physics Master Edgar Martin, who had been responsible for the school having an orchestra.

On the other side of the Atlantic another musical event was unfolding In the previous year Decca Records had signed another future – and sadly short lived - icon of pop, the 20 yr old Buddy Holly. Due to the terms of his contract, his creativity was stifled to the point that he had to release his first blockbuster "That'll be the day" in the name of his band the Crickets in 1957. Decca did not renew the contract and a string of multi million sale hits followed, including "Peggy Sue", "Raining in my Heart" - and for me his greatest, the rousing "Oh Boy!". Then, in February 1959, at the tender age of 22, he was dead, killed in a plane crash along with two other pop stars of the times, The Big Bopper and Richie Valens (just 17), on their way from Iowa to Minnesota for a gig.

I truly believe that Buddy Holly would have been bigger than the Beatles had he lived. Even the Rolling Stones had their first hit with the Holly Number "Not Fade Away" It is said that the Beatles named themselves in honour of the Holly backing group the Crickets. Holly was inducted into the Rock and Roll Hall of Fame in 1989 as one of the top 10 most influential figures in pop music of all time. In 2011 his widow used one of his shoes to place his footprint into the Stars Walk of Fame in Hollywood. RIP Buddy.

The 1957 Oscars produced a surprise win for us Brits. "Bridge on the River Kwai" with Alec Guinness and William Holden scooped Best Picture at the Oscars. Guinness got Best Actor. Another film of prominence that year was "Peyton Place" starring Lana Turner – a bit like film mimicking real life there given her reputation Reputations were also to the fore where Jerry Lee Lewis and Chuck Berry were concerned. They were the Bad boy end of popular music in the late 50s. Jerry Lee was a poor farmer's boy from the backwoods of Louisiana. Born in 1935, he came to be known as the First Great Wild Man of Rock and Roll. He styled his act as "Jerry and his Pumping piano". He did not so much play it as abuse it. He would jump up and down on the ivories, dance on top of it, throw the stool into the crowd and play standing up – at one concert he actually set fire to it! Appropriate in a way, as his seminal work, which will never fade and die, was the crazily played "Great Balls of Fire".

Others followed – "Whole lotta shaking going on", "High School Confidential." are the best known. He became a very rich man almost overnight in '57. Then in 1958 he went and married his cousin Myra – who was aged just 13. Such marriages were legal in the State of Mississippi. And considered an abomination just about everywhere else in the civilised world. When the age of Myra became known, Jerry Lee was reviled in the Press on both sides of the Atlantic. When he attempted a UK Tour in 1959 audiences booed him off the stage wherever he went. His career collapsed – and never really recovered. He still performs at US Concerts to this day. He and Myra were divorced long ago.

Then there was Chuck Berry. Compared to him, Jerry Lee was a choirboy. Born in 1926 - into a middle class African-American family in St Louis – he was sentenced to 3 years for Armed Robbery in 1944 whilst still a High School student. In 1955 he met with the late great Muddy Waters, generally considered the Great Grandfather of the Blues, who inspired him to sign up with a record company. Great works followed - "Roll over Beethoven", "Maybelline", "Johnny be Good". His star faded at the beginning of the 60s – not helped any by being sentenced to 3 years in prison in 1962 for transporting a minor (a girl of 14) over State lines.

They sure liked young flesh those Southern boys!

Ironically the number by which he will be best remembered today, "My ding a ling", an extremely sexually suggestive number, was not recorded until 1972. It was his only US Number One hit.

Chuck is still performing at Concerts across America at the age of 85.

There was one other performer who came to the fore this year. An honourable mention must go to Paul Anka, the Canadian born songwriter, who burst on to the pop scene in 1957 at the tender age of 16 with "Diana", a song he wrote and performed himself. The record has sold in total over 9 million copies, and the song is still played on radio stations across the UK and North America to this day. Anka went on to become one of the leading songwriters of the 20th Century. He was 72 this year and is still working.

*

Momentous events continued to occupy the headlines globally in 1957.

In January Anthony Eden resigned due to chronic ill health brought about in large part by the Suez fiasco. Everyone expected his Deputy Rab Butler to replace him, but the Cabinet chose instead the rather more patrician 60 year old Harold McMillan. Butler served in his Government but never forgave the party for their choice. Leading to the continuing witticism that circulated ever afterwards amongst the political cognoscenti of the time: "*Every time Macmillan flies back into Britain from a foreign visit Rab Butler rushes down to the airport to greet him, and to shake him warmly by the throat.*"

Harold Macmillan achieved a place in history when a few months later he uttered those famous words by which he will always be remembered, when he told the British people that they "had never had it so good". Except he never said that. What he actually said was somewhat less snappy – "*Some of our people have never had it so good, but such prosperity can only be sustained by restraint and common sense*" Just goes to prove that people hear what they want to hear and remember what they want to remember.

In March 1957 petrol rationing ended again, this time after it's brief return the previous year due to the Suez crisis. A month later the Driving Test was re-introduced. The age of Big Oil in the UK that we live in today had dawned.

In September the US Government sent troops to little Rock Arkansas after the State Governor had refused to abide by a Supreme Court ruling that effectively ended the "apartheid" of schools in the State. Nine coloured students could then attend classes.

In October the Soviets launched Sputnik, the first high orbit Earth satellite, sparking a Space War with the US.

Another thing that would come to engage the attention of the US Government of the day was the rise in Britain of the completely misguided and pacifist Campaign for Nuclear Disarmament or CND. CND held their first major rally when they marched on the Aldermaston Atomic Weapons Research Establishment in Easter 1958, and went on to be a thorn in the side of Governments, the MOD - and the Left wing of the Labour Party - for the next 25 years. The US saw Britain as an "unsinkable aircraft carrier" and were appalled that if CND ever achieved its objective then a pillar of the NATO Alliance would be no more and Britain would swiftly become a Moscow satellite state. That this never happened is proved by the fact that this book is written in English.

The 51 Bus route was served by the old red London Transport double decker. It had a two man crew, the driver and the conductor or "clippy" who sold and checked the tickets before clipping them with a small silver punch around his or her neck. We had bus passes. In Term time the 51 served more or less as the Chis and Sid school bus between 7.30 AM and 8.30 AM Mondays to Friday. There was usually only one sartorial colour to be seen on the Upper Deck between those times - the purple of our school blazers. All sorts of shenanigans went on after the conductor had checked our bus passes and retreated to the bottom deck.

Caps were torn from heads and thrown around the compart-
ment. satchels "stolen", scarves held out of the windows. The
smaller boys were tormented - and sometimes worse – by the
larger. The First Years were however - thankfully - too large to
fit through the windows. It was always an eventful ride. A rite of
passage for the new boys.

The real test though came at the end of the journey, or the beginning of the return journey, at the Bus Stops just before Hurst
Road. The game was always the same – how soon before the bus
stopped could you get off it by leaping on to the pavement off
the wide platform at the back while it was still moving - and how
long could you leave it after the bus had pulled away from the
opposite stop before jumping on again, desperately grasping at
the handrail as the only way to prevent you falling flat on your
face in the roadway. I was really quite good at this – my regret
was that dear old Milton could not see my athletic agility.

The small shop in the arcade by the return bus stop was of
course very well frequented by us. Sherbet dips were all the rage
in those days, together with "gob stoppers" large round and
striped mint humbugs. The 1950s and 1960s represented THE
Golden age of toffee and fudge.

Tour de Sidcup

For my 14th birthday in 1957 Dad bought me a Claud Butler
Racing Bike. It had drop handlebars – of course – a 5 speed
Derailleur gearbox with a double clanger, giving 10 separate
speed ratios – naturally - and it had the famed CB lightweight
frame. This was considered to be the Rolls Royce of bicycles in
the 1950s. I was a very lucky lad. The bike changed my life and
opened up new vistas.

Road traffic was still very light in the 50s – less than 3 million
vehicles on the road in toto. The best trip time I ever recorded

was from Meopham in Kent to home in just under an hour. Cross country to Darenth Country Park, then fast down A225/ 224 to the old School Building at Crittalls Corner, tailgating buses and lorries on the way to gain slipstream advantage. (This was 1957, so lorries were not the long 16 wheeled artics of today, with air brakes, but more like large motorised horses and carts that trundled along averaging maybe 40 - 45 mph themselves.) Then I turned off towards St Mary Cray and thence to home. A tiny tad over 20 miles. My parents would have taken the bike away from me had they known the risks I took on it.

Home to Chis and Sid was around 7 miles, and in the summer I often cycled to school. A lot of us did. In the Sixth Form we went to Dartford Girls' Grammar School for ballroom dancing lessons one or two evenings a month (oh, how the World was different then!) This was a 7 mile journey from school.

So let's get this straight. In one day – 7 miles to school, another 7 to Dartford, then back again. Almost 30 miles in total. This was quite normal – most of us with decent bikes could and regularly did easily achieve that in a day. And yet dear old Milton STILL thought I could not possibly be fit unless I stood on my head three times a week!!

(You couldn't cycle the exact same route today even if you wanted to. Not that anyone who valued their own skin would want to. In 1957 there were fewer than 3 million vehicles on the road. Now there are 35 million. Many of them 16 wheeled articulated lorries!)

Fags

Smoking was all the rage in the 1950s. On June 27th 1957 a report from the Medical Research Council linking smoking to lung cancer appeared in The Times. Few paid it much heed at the time – for in 1957 everyone smoked. Fathers and Mothers, Husbands and Wives, Grannies and Granddads, Teenagers and Girlfriends; they smoked at the office, on the factory floor, at home, in Restaurants, in the cinema, at the Theatre, on trains, in planes – they puffed away everywhere and anywhere and pretty much endlessly. The cigarette companies encouraged the kids to smoke as soon as they were old enough by putting glossy cards of the Kings and Queens of England in their parents' fag packets and exhorting them to put them in order so as to collect the whole set.

In the US the cigarette companies used cards of baseball heroes instead I have even seen some old Newsreel adverts in which REAL DOCTORS advocate smoking as being good for you. But then nicotine is more addictive than heroin, so most felt it was. I am pretty sure that if a low flying aircraft had passed across Britain on any fine, airless day in the 50s they would have been able to see the thin blue haze of cigarette smoke covering the land.

I can actually remember when I had my first "ciggie" I was coming back from a Scouting evening with Andrew Dorė along Chislehurst Road when I was about 15, and he offered me a Woodbine. I finally gave up 7 years ago.

The 1950s and 1960s were also the golden years for Pipe Smokers. Every town had at least one or two Tobacconists shops that in addition to maybe 50 or 60 different brands of cigarettes also sold every one of the very many different mixes of Pipe tobacco in pouches or just loose. They also made up mixes to order. You could smell their aromas as soon as you walked in the shops. It was a heady heavy sort of a smell. Then there were pipe cleaners, pipes themselves and smokers accessories. Lighters and cigarette cases – I once owned a silver cigarette box in the late 60s and felt very chic.

Smoking was a very profitable business indeed in those days.

In September 1957 my class year going forward was split into 3 streams. These were Lower Five Modern, focussing on Languages and Literature, Lower Five Science on Science and Maths, and Lower 5 G who supplied half of the School Ist XV Rugby team. This made little difference to the curriculum, it was simply a question of emphasis. As stated earlier, Pedley's sole aim was to get as many placements as possible of C&S boys into Oxbridge. Traditionally Oxbridge had until that time always put more emphasis on the Humanities (Languages, Philosophy, Literature) at the expense of Science. But the world was changing, and I guess he must have felt that a mix of candidate types would give him a better shot. Who knows?

Within LVM we split further into Latin or German – I leapt at German, having developed a palpable distaste for "De Bello Gallico" and six different declinations: Nominative, Accusative, Dative, Genitive, Ablative and Vocative. (I still shudder as I remember them.) German only has 4. Piece of cake.

Our German Master was Mr "Todd" Stringer. He was a decent bloke, slim and shortish, with a pencil moustache. and we all got on well together. He played cricket for the Masters against the boys. I have a group photo of the Masters team. In this he bears a rather worrying likeness to a certain leader of Germany in a blazer and cricketing whites — but it was of course just an illusion?

One big thing in his favour is that he drove an immaculate chocolate brown Singer Hunter. Not a Mercedes.

By this time we were all 14+ and well into adolescence. The School never kept class rosters from the 50s. So together with my old classmate and good friend John Baker we tried to compile a list of our classmates in the Lower Fifth. We turned out to be a pretty eclectic bunch.

First up there was Malcolm Fitzearle (who I understand now lives in Vancouver and is a world authority on Grizzly Bears – and on Parisian toilets in the 1950s!) Then there was Harry Schofield, who became a Policeman,. Other contemporaries in Year 4 were Tony Skinner, Paul Eley (who even at that age screamed Bank Manager at you), Graham Sargent., Ernie Crisp, a very shy and timid boy, Geoff Newman and Tommy Callaghan, Will Smith and James Chilton. (Both Orpington boys, I remember that they each developed a yen for restoring old Riley cars after leaving school).

Huggett went on to play bridge for England. Mervyn Kerswell was a lugubrious lad. Tall and skinny with pebble glasses his ambition in life was to become an Actuary. You do not get more boring than that! Then there was McDowell. Poor chap suffered from epilepsy. I never witnessed him have a *Grand Mal* but I do remember that he would sometimes have a *Petit Mal* while sitting at his desk. His head would go down on to the desk, his face would go into a rictus and he would tremble and twitch uncontrollably. The best thing one could do was to ignore him at such a time. I do know that the Masters had been given advice on how to handle a worse fit. Don't let him swallow his tongue. You had to feel sorry for him.

There was also Smith TR, the short-sighted Rugby player - just ponder on that for a moment - as well as Terry Button, who apparently went on to serve in MI6 and then later became the Sheriff of the State of Victoria in Australia. I should also give a mention to James Adair, known as "Scottie" because he had such a thick Scottish accent nobody could understand a word he said. I really mean this. When asked where in Scotland he came from he would reply "Renfrewshire" – at least that's what I think he said

One or two classmates qualify for a special mention. Martin Donnelly became a hero in one English lesson in the Lower 5th when he was asked by Walshie to compose a poem ad lib. A new TV Western series, "Bronco Lane", starring Ty Hardin, had appeared on our screens in 1958. The theme tune ran as follows "Bronco Bronco tearing across the Texas plain, Bronco Bronco Bronco Lane". Unfortunately (for the series) there was also a toilet paper named Bronco being advertised at the same time. Donnelly came up with the following ditty - "Bronco Bronco tearing along the dotted line. Bronco Bronco just in time". We all fell about. Donnelly got a detention from Walsh for taking the mickey!

Then there was the boy - who shall remain nameless - who allegedly won points for ingenuity for having invented a good way to pass internal exams. When he got the marked papers back he would extract a section and replace it with the same section that he had completed afterwards at home. He would then announce to the teacher that part of his work had not been marked. (You would need the same pen and the same writing paper but I suppose you could get away with it once or twice.) Want to bet he ended up as a Merchant Banker?.

Lastly there was the outrageous way that Graham Sargent used to bully poor timid Ernie Crisp. Sending a very shy boy like him down to the Chemist for a packet of three condoms really was a bit strong Shocking – but hilarious!!

*

Anyhow, my marks for the year continued to put me in mid table. Not worthy of praise from Pedley during his termly inspections, but enough to avoid the harsher sanctions he gave to those threatened by relegation. German was not proving to be an easy alternative to Latin, but at least I was now learning a language still spoken in the outside world.

By now I was 14yrs and 5 months, and so considered mature enough for sex education. This was dispensed by Doc King in the Biology lab. To a constant background of titters and sniggers from the back of the room he described the sexual act by means of some very graphic diagrams. A few boys blushed furiously, one or two turned pale, but the most affected was Carter (*not his real name, for reasons that will become clear.*). He was a big lump of a lad and had been perched on one of the high lab stools. As the diagrams became ever more graphic, he suddenly fainted clean away at the enormity of it all and crashed to the ground. We all laughed loudly.

Carter was a bit thick, let's be honest. Although he was actually quite well developed for his age. This fact had once led several lads in our year to carry out a rather drastic form of Biology practical with him as the guinea pig. They took him across the school field into the woods where they performed a sex act on him just to see the result. (No I am not making this up – teenage boys can be some of the cruellest creatures on the planet.) I do not think I could ever have been party to such an act – although had I known about it at the time who knows.

Chis and Sid was of course boys only, and it was not that uncommon for boys at the back of the class to play with themselves during lessons. Sometimes – how can I put this delicately? - we would admire and compare each others' nascent manhoods. Yes - this too is true! It is easy to understand from this behaviour how Boys only Boarding Schools can sometimes breed homosexuality. No way would it have happened in mixed sex classes – but in the case of us 14 yr old boys, it was the first faltering step in the journey through puberty into manhood.

One boy in my year – no names, no pack drill – reached the end of this journey rather earlier than the rest of us. He obviously did not pay sufficient attention to Doc either. Just a very few years later, despite the free availability of condoms from the local chemist or barber, he made his girl friend pregnant. Today, the girl would probably have been on the pill so it would not even have happened. Errors can be rectified by an abortion. Conversely the DSS would probably give the couple a Council flat as well as providing maternity benefit, and Social Services would shower them with all sorts of goodies.

But this was the 1950s – abortion was illegal, and such "unhappy" things were simply swept under the carpet. The boy was warned off by her parents, who then adopted the baby as their own. She then presumably grew up believing that her Mother was in fact her big sister. It must have happened a lot. Another preferred option for the better off was for the girl to disappear "to the Colonies" for a year. Then return with the sad tale of how she had married a big game hunter who had promptly been trampled by an elephant, leaving her a young tearful widow with a child.

I remember one girl from a very good family, in a road near to ours on the Knoll Estate, who returned from Spain with a baby and a similar story of how she had been "widowed" (Maybe he had been gored by a bull in the ring at *Las Ventas* in Madrid?) More likely it was bull shit. Yes, shame still meant something special when I was growing up.

In the 1950s the only alternative to the above social deceits was for the couple to marry. Not possible if each of them was still at school!

So although the permissive Sixties were just around the corner, the Church and the morality of the times saw to it that most girls were "good girls" and were virgins when they got married.

(But happily not always virginal, for the turmoil of teenage hormones was no less then than it is now and ever will be amen). Although perhaps the most pragmatic reason had been the the very real fear of the shame and ignominy that would follow an unwanted pregnancy. They would be branded a scarlet woman, shunned by any future suitor.

The World was still a very different place in the 1950s.

*

For instance, in those days there were no drunken sluts to be found lying on the pavements of our High Streets on Friday or Saturday nights as there are now, with their legs in the air and flashing their knickers - or lack of them – at passers by. (Aside from any other consideration, young women were brought up to have more respect for themselves.) Another more practical consideration had been that the only place to buy a drink in those days was in a Pub – of which there were many tens of thousands around the country. In those days, even in the swinging 60s that followed, women did not go into pubs on their own or in groups – only whores did that. They had to be accompanied by men. They never ordered drinks at the Bar.

Pubs closed early by law. At 10.20.publicans would call "Last orders please." You rushed to the Bar to get a drink. You then had 10 minutes to finish it, before being shown off the premises (The Publican had no choice – in those days most policemen patrolled on foot and each had his own small population of pubs to check on. If he was found serving after hours he could lose his licence – if people were just found drinking in his pub he could also.)

Yes - a very different place.

*

In November 1957, at the age of 19, another giant of pop music from the US, Eddy Cochrane, published his only album in his lifetime. Born in Minnesota in October 1938, he was killed in a car crash on the A4 in Chippenham in Wiltshire on his way to a gig on 17th April 1960. Like Buddy Holly, he too died tragically young in pursuit of his art, and also left behind him a legacy of music that is still played today. Since his death over 50 years ago his music has been inspirational to and performed by Groups as diverse as The Beatles, Led Zeppelin and the Sex Pistols. Had he and Buddy Holly been alive throughout the 60s, the world of pop music in the ensuing decades would surely have been very different. Very different.

Eddy's style of music was so optimistic, so uplifting. His classic numbers include "C'mon everybody", "Something else", and perhaps his most famous of all "Summertime Blues".

Buddy Holly, Eddy Cochrane, Elvis, Jerry Lee, Chuck, Paul Anka - we teenagers of the late 1950s and early 60s were truly blessed.

*

At school Masters came and went. I learnt what follows only recently after reading the excellent History of the School "Past Purple", written by Charles Wells and John Hazelgrove, two former Masters who joined the staff in 1975 and 1981 respectively. Although therefore what follows is naked plagiarism I feel that as I was actually there at the time I can claim seniority. It says everything about Pedley and his obsession with Oxbridge.

Apparently in 1957 Pedley had clandestinely taken one of the new staff intake, Alastair Wilson, aside and given him a list of 30 boys whom he instructed Wilson to "fast track" as Form Master through O levels a year early. "I want all these boys to go to Oxford or Cambridge" he told Wilson. 22 eventually made it.

Had this been widely known at the time, it would have been very demoralising for the rest of the School, and I am sure would have elicited angry responses from many of the parents. Not the least because all of us boys had already passed the 11+ to get to the school on merit. To then be subject to the clandestine and arbitrary decisions of an obsessive leader was a betrayal of trust. How had these boys been chosen? How could one man fast track a class in eight subjects? How much of the school's resources were devoted to "Headmaster's arbitrary favourites".?

This angers me even now on principle – but does not surprise me unduly. It just reinforces my view of Pedley as a poor leader and a flawed man. A man who commanded respect but never earned it.

With that fact in mind, the book "Past Purple" also tells the story of Eric Side, a Science Master at the school. He coined the name "Moby Dick" for Pedley in the Staff Common Room, after his whale like size and pompous nature. *"Thar she blows."* he would whisper to his colleagues as Pedley hove into view.

Genius!

1958

I vividly remember that it was during a History lesson with Nobby Clarke that the news of the Munich air crash reached the school On the afternoon of 6th February 1958 BEA Flight 609 with 36 passengers and six crew on board caught fire shortly after take off from Munich airport. and crashed in flames. The flight had been taking the Manchester United football team and a group of Sports journalists back to the UK after a European Cup game against Bayern Munich.

Seven First Team players of the squad known as "The Busby Babes", with an average age of just 24, died in the crash – Roger Byrne, the Team captain, Mark Jones, Eddie Colman, Tommy Taylor, Liam Whelan, David Pegg and Geoff Bent. Eight journalists and six Club officials also perished. 15 days later Duncan Edwards, their star player, considered to have been one of the best mid-fielders ever to have played the game, and the youngest player ever to play for England up until then, died of his injuries in hospital in Munich.

The terrible tragedy hit the nation very hard. The Queen sent a personal message of sympathy to the families of the dead, and to the Club. Every one in football mourned their deaths. Man United still hold a Minute's Silence whenever they are playing at home on the anniversary of the event. As a supporter of Liverpool, who remember their own tragedy at Hillsborough every year, I can appreciate their sense of loss more than 50 years on.

The subsequent Air Accident Investigation team found that ice on the wings had caused the crash. I remembered this solemnly again one winter's evening a few years ago when my flight back to London from Franz Joseph Strauss, the new airport outside Munich that opened around 15 years ago, was delayed. Our plane had sat on the stand for over an hour when it should have been in the air. Then the pilot announced that due to the cold weather they were going to have to to de ice the wings. My first thought was – take your time!

*

1958 was also the year that Sixth Formers got their own design of cap to distinguish them from the rest. Prefects got a a golden tassel on theirs – another attempt by Pedley to make the school look like Eton.

Another much happier event of 1958 was the formation of The School Film Society. Its first showing was "The Lavender Hill Mob" that seminal Ealing Comedy starring Alec Guinness, Stanley Holloway, and two who would go on to even bigger things on the small screen: Sid James and Alfie Bass.

Across in Hollywood "Gigi" with Leslie Caron and Maurice Chevalier won best Picture at the Oscars. This was a double first – a European film with French co stars. A worthy contender was "Cat on a Hot Tin Roof" with Paul Newman and Elizabeth Taylor. David Niven won best Actor for "Separate tables." Doubtless as always he had played himself. He was much more noted for his charm than for his dramatic potential.

Paris

Everyone has heard of "The Red Baron" Manfred von Richthofen, and of the legless Battle of Britain Fighter pilot ace Douglas Bader. But unless you are French, you have probably never heard of Georges Guynemer. He was a French fighter ace of World War 1, who had over 50 confirmed kills until he went missing in action towards the end of 1917. (*No cheese eating surrender monkey there, George!*) He was one of the few Frenchmen to win both the Croix de Guerre and the Legion d' Honneur. There is a street named after him in Paris – it runs down the eastern side of the *Jardin du Luxembourg*. In that street there is the school that bears his name, *the Lycèe Guynemer*. It was here our French group stayed on my first visit to France at Easter 1958.

Taffy Jenkins was in charge of our group. It was the first time I had ever seen an armed Policeman. The *Jardin du Luxembourg* was patrolled by gendarmes with their *"mitraillettes"* slung over their shoulders. For this was the height of the Algerian War of Independence – and the *Jardin,* a public park, surrounds the *Palais du Luxembourg* – the home of the French Senate. Just a few weeks before our visit an Algerian nationalist had been shot dead trying to break through the security cordon. They were troubled times for France.

Since 1952 the FLN, the Algerian terrorist group / freedom fighters according to your point of view, had been carrying out atrocities in their homeland. Recently they had been targeting the Colonial Police. A few months before the FLN had become active in Metropolitan France Although they had not yet started attacking the Gendarmes in France, in March 1958 7,000 police had demonstrated in Paris demanding greater powers. Then one of their right wing members - a certain Jean Marie le Pen - led a march of 20,000 people to the Elysèe Palace. Two months later the 4th Republic collapsed and early in 1959 De Gaulle became President and announced the 5th Republic.

A few months later De Gaulle did a volte face and announced that he would support Independence for Algeria. His Government had estimated that the French farmers and land-owners in the country, known as "les pieds noirs" or black feet, would largely stay on after independence. Instead of which, in fear of their lives, tens of thousands of them and their families just upped sticks and left for Metropolitan France.

The Army in Algeria rebelled, and its leaders under General *Massu* planned a *coup d' ètat.* Paratroopers from Algiers even "occupied" Corsica. De Gaulle made a patriotic broadcast and the majority of the armed forces in France itself stayed loyal. The rebels finally stood down. *Massu* fled to Spain where he established the *"L'Armèe de l' Organisation Secrète"* or OAS, sworn to kill De Gaulle and retake Algeria. (as set out in the film "The Day of the Jackal")

Paris was a revelation for me when I made my first visit in 1958. No buildings had been destroyed in World War 2. The city had fallen unscathed to the Wehrmacht in 1940. In 1944 the German Governor of Paris, General Dietrich von Chollitz, is said to have been ordered by Hitler to "leave Paris in ruins" before retreating. He apparently disobeyed this order, and was credited with preventing a total uprising by treating with the Resistance before marching his men away back to Germany. The Eiffel Tower, the Pantheon, the Louvre, Notre Dame and all the other priceless architectural treasures remained unscathed, preserved for future Generations.

But as a 15 year old I was more exercised by the toilet facilities in the school. These consisted of a hole in the tiled floor with hand rails that served for – well, every function. One hole per dormitory. I remember Malcolm Fitzearle at first refusing to use it, demanding better facilities. I don't blame him. The dormitory where we were billeted was freezing cold. There was no hot water – maybe they had heard of English public schools? I remember we made visits to the Eiffel Tower, the *Conciergerie*, and the *Place de la Concorde*. We also climbed the winding stone staircase that led to the roof terrace of the great Cathedral of Notre Dame. I clearly remember dropping a 5 centime coin down onto the forecourt. I chose it as it weighed almost nothing, but I hope nobody was injured!

We marched up and down the *Champs Elysees* to the *Arc de Triomphe*. Our crocodile of British 15 yr olds wound in and out of Metro stations. These seemed universally run down and neglected. In that era they still had the hydraulic doors at the entries to the platforms that closed when a train was due. On the Metro every carriage had seats marked "*Reservé mutilés de guerre*" - Reserved for war wounded." They were everywhere. From previous wars, and from the current conflict in Algeria. One legged men on crutches, one armed men, blind men, disfigured men. A sad testament to glory. The other two signs that were everywhere were "*Défense d'afficher*" - No Bill Sticking – and "*Défense de cracher*"– No Spitting. The latter seemed to be largely ignored.

Breakfast at the Lycee was the classic of the period. The *Cafe au lait* was served in those uniquely French breakfast cups you will no longer find in France – broad cups with twin handles and shallow sides that more resembled soup bowls. Fresh baguettes with butter and jam. No croissants for school boys! The packed lunches we were given were also a bit different to Blighty. Baguette, butter, hard boiled egg, a slice or two of ham or some other *charcuterie*, or maybe garlic salami. And then there were the omnipresent *cornichons*. Crunchy little pickled gherkins. Apart from the bread and eggs all of the latter were new treats for our English tastebuds.

We ate in the refectory at the school. For dinner there might have been a piece of strong *Pâté de Campagne* or fish soup, followed by fish or chicken. One evening we were were served what the French call *(bif)steck frites*. The meat was rather tough – and had very probably been pulling a milk cart around London until a few weeks before. Horse meat was widely used in French cuisine at that time – and in some places still is. Dartmoor ponies are sold for the butchers' trade to this day.

I had first learned – extremely rudimentary – French at St Nicholas when I was 4. Here I was trying it out with basic questions to passers by on the Metro or in the street. Parisians are famously rude, even to the rest of the French; which I soon discovered. Most of them also seemed to be smoking *Gaulloises* and the foul smelling *Gitanes* of the time with the yellowish cigarette paper. The men had developed the trick of allowing the cigarette to droop loosely from the bottom lip, attached just by the spittle to the flesh. My Father rolled his own, but this still looked particularly revolting by comparison. I remember one *"faux pas"* I made – by addressing an adult using *"Tu"* the familiar form of the word "you" used only between family and friends – and to children and animals. He could tell I was not French, and therefore naturally ignorant, and grunted a reply. I fell hopelessly in love with France that week. The French would take a lot longer.

Trainspotting.

I now have a confession to make – between the ages of around 13 – 15 I was an avid train spotter. I put it down to the fact that there was so little else for an inquisitive mind to do in the 1950s. A group of us used to take the footpath that led underneath the railway and then walk to the footbridge over the up line. Here we would take out our books of holy writ – the latest publication from Ian Allan Books listing all the locos and their numbers in the Southern region.

The Southern Railway suburban network was electrified in the 1930s. We were not really interested in those trains. What we were pledged to do was to record every one of the steam loco-motives listed in the book. The most famous of all the trains that passed along the Down Line through Orpington was the Golden Arrow Boat Train that left Victoria for Dover and the Channel Ferry to Calais, where it met a direct connection on to Paris *Gare du Nord*. Often pulled by the Battle of Britain Class 4-6-2 "Sir Winston Churchill", it would thunder under the bridge pulling its distinctive yellow sided Pullman coaches behind it and disappear off towards Sevenoaks and the sea. The sound and the fury: the hiss of the steam, the billowing clouds of smoke and occasional shower of sparks from the funnel, the smell of burning coal – this was nirvana for us nerds.

As our passion grew for train numbers we moved further afield, buying the Ian Allan books on all the steam locos in Britain. We began spotting on the platforms of the major London Termini - Western Region out of Paddington, LNER out of Liverpool Street and London and Northern out of Kings Cross. At Paddington we attempted to tick off from the listings every one of the magnificent King Class locos, universally agreed to be the most beautiful locos ever built. At Liverpool Street there were the Castle locos, and at Kings Cross – well I forget but more steam

Even this did not satisfy our lust for yet more numbers. So we began to resort to trespass – to catch the trains while they were parked. The main Train Shed for the Southern region was at Nine Elms in South London. The main shed for Western region was at Old Oak Common just outside Paddington. The main shed for the LNER was at Kentish Town. Our group brazenly found a way in to them all and calmly walked around taking down numbers.

The first thing we discovered was that we were not alone. The Depots seemed to be swarming with us nerds. Most of the railwaymen turned a blind eye to our presence. God alone knows how many things we would be charged with in our present wonderful, caring and modern "Democracy" for our presence then - everything from suspicion of terrorism through criminal trespass to breaches of 'Elf and Safety: oh yes the world is a very different place today.

None of us as far as I know has ever ticked off all the numbers in the Ian Allan books. I eventually grew tired of shinning over fences at railway sheds and gave up the game.

*

It was also in 1958 that an event occurred that would eventually put a big and permanent dent in Rail travel. The then Minister of Transport Ernest Marples opened the Preston Bypass, the first operational stretch of Motorway in Britain. I remember watching the opening on TV. The ribbon was cut and a whole phalanx of cars (about 8 of them) set off along it. How things have changed. The road is now part of the M6 and whenever I am driving north along it to watch Liverpool at Anfield I still carry that memory of a deserted motorway in my mind: as I sit in the eternal queues south of the M62 Intersection. Progress is clearly relative!

One of the more flagrant abuses inflicted on us by the school was Cross Country running. Changing into shorts and vests on a cold winter's day and running three miles through wet grass and the woods beyond was made just bearable by stopping en route to ogle the girls in the Drama school across the lake. My chum Colin was pretty good at Cross Country, once coming 5th out of around a hundred (I often came around 95th) but he too soon realised the futility of it all and would decamp to the Groundsman's hut to share a Woodbine with those stalwarts of the School Rugby 1st XV Link Patching and Staples.

I had realised the futility from Day One, so invented the new field sport of cross country tramping, making sure I splashed through muddy puddles and smeared mud up my legs. Then I would valiantly cross the line red faced and out of breath like a brave soldier. (In the 6th Form several of us would decamp in our running kit to the nearby "Black Horse" pub in Blackfen to slake our thirst. On wet days the Public Bar was a bit like the 6th Form Common Room.)

The second half of my year in LV Modern was taken up by revising for mock O levels. Which I sat in November. We were in the Assembly Hall invigilated by masters. Prognosis was mixed.

*

At Speech Day in December 1958 Pedley gave a rant against Comprehensive Education. Many Education Authorities were sabotaging the system of excellence set by Grammar schools. It was the thin end of the wedge. In retrospect, this was one of the very few things that Pedley ever said that I agreed with in 7 years at the school

*

As I reached 15 I gave up train spotting and my social circle began to grow dramatically. I became close pals with John Sachs, who lived round the corner in Keswick Road. His Father was a Solicitor and a very dour man. The very first time I knocked on John's door his Father opened it. The conversation was short and to the point. After finding out who I was and what I wanted he said to wait, then shut the door again in my face saying "The house will get cold" and went off to find his son. I never saw him smile. John was the exact opposite of his Father – happy go lucky, very good company with classic good looks that attracted the girls.

Around the corner in Irene Road lived the Cornish boys. Their house had large grounds at the back which fell away with stepped lawns down to a pond at the bottom. Ideal for hide and seek and rough and tumbles. (When I returned to Orpington last year after 30+ years away, I found that their house had gone and those lawns had morphed into a small circle of houses named Sequoia Gardens)

At the end of Irene Road lived Nick. His house had a large garden with a huge garden hammock swing. John and I spent many a lazy summer afternoon in his garden in 1959 and 1960. Whilst sipping lemonade brought by his Mother, a charming Welsh lady who always looked unflappable We listened over and over again to Buddy Holly. My strongest memory though was in 1960, listening to the new hit sensation from Roy Orbison "Only the lonely". In keeping with the respectability of the area, his Father was Chief Secretary to the Church Commissioners. A very important post in an age when the Church of England had a far greater influence on the nation as a whole than it does now. As well as much more wealth.

I must confess I could never really fathom Nick. On the face of it he had it all. He was at Sevenoaks School as a day boy, was tall athletic with saturnine good looks – yet somehow he had a chip on his shoulder about something. I could never figure what it was. It made him a bit unapproachable to many of our contemporaries. He could be quite cold with people on occasion – even with John and I and we were all three of us pretty close. Maybe he was expected to be more pious than the rest of us due to his old man's position. Who knows?

Nick had an older sister. She was a tall good looking blonde girl – must have been late teens or even early 20s. He used to tell us that most of his sex education had been based on doing a peeping Tom on her when she was on the sofa with her boyfriend. This became the subject of much fantasising by us teenage lads. *Perverts? Us? Never!*

I remember the days the three of us used to spend in Petts Wood woods, alongside Chislehurst Road. The main London railway line ran alongside them and there was a pedestrian Level Crossing. (As to whether we played chicken against oncoming trains – I couldn't possibly comment.) One of the clearest and most humorous memories I have of John was a few days before Guy Fawkes night one year. He was wearing a thick Canadian lumberjack's jacket with deep pockets, in which he had fireworks that he had bought earlier. Somehow, his roll- up cigarette must have fallen into that pocket – the sight of him running around in circles, showering Technicolour sparks, as a Roman candle went off in his pocket, followed by a banger, while he desperately tried to wriggle out of his jacket will always stay with me. Needless to say he got no sympathy from Nick or me. We laughed ourselves sick! John emerged from this unscathed though reeking of black powder. The jacket was a write-off.

These woods also contain a lasting memorial to a man whose 8 years of dogged persistence, from 1907 until his death in 1915, led – quite literally - to the increased enlightenment of all of us in Britain. A man whose name has long since been completely forgotten - except by the people of Petts Wood. He was William Willett, a builder, who was the man who conceived British Summer Time, and then spent the rest of his life lobbying the Great and the Good for its introduction. He had wanted to put the clocks forward 80 minutes so that he could enjoy life with his family on summer evenings.

He endlessly lobbied the powers that were until it finally became a political issue spurred on by the need to conserve fuel in the First World War. The Bill to put the clocks forward 60 minutes in summer passed into law in 1917 – sadly two years after Willett had died. So he never got to enjoy his extra time in the sun as we all have ever since.

It was also in these same woods that Dad and I used to forage for various types of mushrooms and toadstools – not for food but to identify those that could kill you. It has been an awful long time since I last did this, but I do recall that any fungus with any part coloured red was a toadstool and should be given a wide berth. I also remember some of the strange names the different species of fungi had: "Buttercap", "Clouded Agaric", "Common Puffball", "Fairies Bonnets". Not all of the names were that twee mind – how can one ever forget the "Dogs Vomit slime mould"?! Some of the dangerous ones are Agaric, Skullcap and Death Cap and their derivatives. These can all kill you and at best make you very ill.

It was about this time that Irene Road itself briefly became the centre of attention. There was a house halfway down before the road bent to the right, alongside yet another alleyway that led down to Broxbourne Common. One morning the lady of the house was doing the ironing, or something similar, when there was a loud rumble and the front garden disappeared into the bowels of the Earth. It had fallen into a *Denehole*.

The underlying base rock in much of Kent is chalk. Many people say that over centuries water running down a seam in the chalk carves out a cave system beneath until the ground is weakened and collapses into it. Others say that they are old excavations made by Stone Age man. Skeletons and artefacts have been found at the base of them – but these could just be from people who had happened to be standing above it as the *Denehole* suddenly opened. So if you are thinking of moving to Kent —

The hole was a source of much curiosity for us locals. I have no idea how they plugged it. It must have been at least 10 metres deep and 5 metres across and stayed untended for some time.

Next time I go back to the "old country" I must see if things have changed in the last 50+ years!

Opposite Irene Road is Cyril Road – do you think that the guy who developed the Knoll area in the 1930s had kids? Another Chis and Sid boy in my year lived here. I shall not name him either. When he was around 15 he was climbing a tree when the branch broke. The branch was over a spiked metal fence. He fell – astraddle the fence! Ye Gods! For the rest of my time at school and beyond I and all my year were asking ourselves - "Did he? "Can he still?"" "Has he?". Never did find out.

It was in the summer of '59 that I started going to the Bickley Lido. You could spend all day there when it was sunny, lounging around on the sun decks smoking a Woodbine and ogling the girls. *You could even go swimming!* One of the main attractions for us lads was Sally Jackson. She had a woman's body even at 15. She sheathed it in a tight fitting one piece blue swimsuit. She was very flirtatious – and was the only English girl of that era that I recall who did not shave her armpits This French habit made her even more alluring.

Inflation

As we all know, this has been the great scourge of the past 60 years. The worse damage was done in the Wilson years of the 1970s, where it recorded a double digit average every year for the entire decade. In 1975 it attained the dizzy heights of 24% pa.

Property price inflation has been even worse / better depending when you bought.

When my parents bought 6 Stanley in 1941 they paid the handsome price of £ 975!!

When my Father died in 1963 the house was valued for probate at £4250

When my Mother remarried in 1977 she sold the house for around £40,000.

Houses in the same road now go for around £450,000.

Income levels have changed just a bit in the past 60 years as well.

The ANNUAL wage of a manual worker averaged around £450 in the early1950s.

The ANNUAL salary of a Manager in private or public Industries was in the region of £1300

The ANNUAL salary of a Doctor was around £ 2,000.

The State Pension for a married couple was around £150 per annum. Equivalent to over £3000 today. (Although you did not get too long to enjoy it. Average life expectancy for a man was 67, for a woman 72)

£1 Premium Bonds had been introduced in 1952. The top prize - £1,000.

Income tax was high – nearly 50%. The cost of living had begun to rise sharply by 1955. Food prices in particular were going up fast now that food rationing had finally been abolished.

A Morris Minor 1000 motorcar cost £700.

A pint of beer cost under a shilling (4.5p today)

A pack of 10 Woodbine cigarettes - 1 shilling (5p)

A score of 26 at darts down the Pub became universally known as Bed and Breakfast – as this was the price it cost in a Guest House for an overnight stay. Two shillings and sixpence. Or half a crown as it was called then. 12. 5p today.

A ten shilling note (50p today) would get you lunch at a top London restaurant with change. —

And the cost of building one complete new Grammar School in 1954? £300,000 - all in!! Yes just Three hundred thousand pounds!Bet you thought it was a lot more than that

Yes the value of money – like life - was very different in the 1950s.

*

Our beloved Headmaster continued to be the butt of cruel humour (*warning, irony breakout!*) You may or may not remember the hot drink called *Bev* that was around in the 50s. "*Relax with Bev*" was their advertising slogan. It was to feature rather prominently in the Annual End of Term School Concert that year. At the time there was no full time School Secretary and Pedley had a temporary stand in. Her name was Beverley Knight - she was young, wore short skirts, and was very fanciable indeed. So what came next was rather inevitable – a Montage sketch from the 6th form featuring the slogan "Headmasters relax with Bev". As per usual Pedley was far from amused.

1959

It must therefore have been a great relief to Pedley when Eileen Butler, Mrs, joined the School at the beginning of the following term as the new, permanent School Secretary. She would hold the post for the next 20 years as it happens. She was a friendly interface between the rest of us and her boss. By this time our beloved Headmaster had acquired a somewhat pejorative nickname – "*Slash.*" This had nothing to do with serial killers – although it might have been appropriate: it seemed to us boys that he certainly possessed the required coldness and indifference to anyone who stood in the way of his objectives. No, it had a rather more unpleasant connotation – so those of a more delicate disposition should avert their gaze now. Think Pedley and piddly. The nickname was "Slash" as in - "I won't be long, I'm just going for a slash"

He remained unaware of this – I guess. Until one day, in the summer term, the Upper V1 (supposedly) placed an advert in the Times – which at that time still had advertising on the front page. This read as follows: "*Ped pig, well smoked, prices slashed. Apply Headmaster Chislehurst and Sidcup Grammar School*" (The "well smoked" referred to the fact that his Study always stank of tobacco smoke.) They then stuck the paper under the door of his study with the relevant ad highlighted.

A lengthy and rigorous campaign of intimidation and reprisals was launched in an attempt to unearth the perpetrators of this heinous crime. As far as I am aware, nobody was ever brought to account. The rest of the school cheered loudly - out of earshot of our beloved leader.

*

We had always had a wind up portable gramophone at home that played old 78rpm vinyl records. The records I remember were old – songs from the musicals, and one particular rendering of "Stormy Weather". Then for my 16th birthday Mum and Dad bought me one of those brand spanking new record players that you plugged into the mains. I can exactly remember the first four records that I bought. The very first was "Stupid Cupid" by Connie Francis (which was top of the Hit Parade at the time.) Then "Splish splash" by Charlie Drake – oh my God what an admission. Third was Adam Faith with his most successful number ever "What do you want".

Faith would go on to become an iconic figure of the Swinging 60s. Number Four was "It's only make believe" by Conway Twitty. Then came Tommy Steele with his smash hit "Singing the Blues". Classics all – well OK maybe not Charlie Drake.

As for Charlie Drake, he went on to have his own Sitcom on the BBC. His catch phrase of "Hello my darlings" became repeated universally. I had no idea – then - of its origin. I have since learned where it came from. Drake was a baby faced very short man - 5ft 1 inch in his socks. He was the most unlikely leading man in films Yet he did make a number of Movies (none of them Oscar material!). During shooting he would stand opposite leading ladies. His eyeline was usually on around the same level as her breasts. You can figure out the rest for yourselves.

*

In the world at large there were several momentous events in 1959. In Britain perhaps the most controversial was the

137

publication by Penguin Books of Lady Chatterley's Lover by D H Lawrence. First published as a "private" edition in Italy as long ago as 1928, it was instantly banned by the Lord Chamberlain's Office as obscene. This would lead to the famous trial at the Old Bailey the following year, the outcome of which would ultimately lead - within two decades mind - to the final ending of Censorship by those whom Orwell called "the striped trousered ones who rule us"

Another important event. for Britain in 1959 was the granting of Independence to Cyprus, thereby ending the bloody insurrection of the pro Greece terrorist group Eoka led by Archbishop Makarios. This had cost the lives of several hundred British troops.

In Cuba, Fidel Castro finally triumphed in the Revolution. driving President Batista out of the country. One dictatorship was replaced by another. *Plus ça change —*

But maybe the seminal event of 1959 had actually been the production by the US company Texas Instruments of the first integrated circuit – the first faltering step towards modern computing, the internet, and everything. Allegedly.

*

At the Oscars in 1959 Best Picture was "Ben Hur" with Charlton Heston, who also took Best Actor. This was the latest – and one of the last – of the Sword and Sandals sagas made famous by Cecil B de Mille. Another cinematic milestone this year – one that has survived the test of time - was the quirky "Some like it Hot" with Marilyn Monroe; and Jack Lemmon in drag!

But for me there was one sad event in film in 1959 – the "Three Stooges" made their 190th – and last – short film. The World would be a sadder place without them *(well, it would!)*

In May we sat our O levels. I was never going to pass Maths – although Mental Arithmetic has always been one of my strong points - and when the results came through in August I hadn't. Struck down by Algebra! Nor had I passed History – I feel I was robbed here, having swotted up in detail on the very questions that were in the Exam papers. 6 out of 8 was OK I guess.

Improvised explosive devices.

In the summer term of 1959 a state of alarm was raised at school after a number of weed killer and sugar pipe bombs were detonated on the school playing fields and in the nearby woods. These were dangerous things that could take your arm off, and sprayed shrapnel in all directions that could have easily killed wildlife or passers-by. Eventually, three boys – Butler, Martin, and Walker – were caught. Surely they were expelled? Not a bit of it – as Pedley considered they had academic ability and might get to Oxbridge. So they just got detentions and strokes of the bamboo cane. At the same time my chum Johnny Baker was summarily expelled – for taking a couple of days off after completing his O levels.

This aptly demonstrates the partisan and arbitrary way Pedley distinguished between those boys HE thought might get to Oxbridge – thereby enhancing his own reputation - and every other boy in the school. For whose educational development he SHOULD have had responsibility. Is it any wonder the man was so widely despised by us boys?

Front row

When it comes to sporting excellence, US colleges give out Sports scholarships and bursaries. So do Oxford and Cambridge - although they vehemently deny it. Patching, Link, Doricott and Staples were the backbone of our School Rugby 1st XV. Pete Staples was in our class. A tall lanky rather laconic lad, he came to school one day that summer with his foot heavily bandaged: he had sliced off his big toe with a motor mower the previous weekend. Living up to his well deserved reputation as a bit of a hard man, he went straight back into Rugby training on the field the following week.

Patching was in Lower 5G - a largely non academic group! He won the hearts of many of the hormonal teenagers in the school when, tiring of a young female Maths Supply Teacher he told her to "go change her jam rag". She fled from the classroom, from the school premises, and never came back. Life was so *straightforward* for the boys of Lower 5G.

They do say that Football is a game for gentlemen played by hooligans, and Rugby is a game for hooligans played by gentlemen. You can see this at any International at Twickenham. Rugby referees are all small wiry men, about 1 metre 60 at best and weighing maybe 60 kilos in their stockinged feet. But on the field every player on both sides, including a fair number of plug uglies weighing at least twice as much and more than him, and towering head and shoulders above him, are genuinely afraid of him. When spoken to harshly by the ref they stand there sheepishly shivering in their socks like naughty 8 year olds.

Soccer referees must be green with envy!!

Johnny Baker played for the school in the Colts XV, at Full Back or on the Wing. We played against a selection of Private and Public schools – Haberdashers Aske's, Coopers, Christs College, Blackheath, Dartford Grammar, Erith Grammar. There was no league table as such, the game was the thing. According to John St Joseph's was the team to beat.

I missed the time when they were playing Dartford Grammar. The ref apparently favoured our opponents and then awarded a dodgy penalty right in front of our posts. As he ran up to take it Patching shouted out a word that was not exactly a blessing – and the kicker missed it. The Ref let him take it again – and he scored.

Graffiti left in the Changing Rooms after the game regarding, amongst other things, the Ref's parentage left no doubts as to what our team felt about this decision. Pedley had the whole team in front of him the next school day and demanded to know who had done it. Only Patching, in a rare display of nobility, owned up to it. He was promptly banned from all sport.

John excelled even more at cricket. He was feared as a demon fast bowler, and went on to play Minor Counties cricket for Caernarvon. He bunked off at the end of the Summer Term after finishing his O levels – and was then expelled, refused access to the 6th form year, and banned from playing cricket for the school as well. Spiteful man Pedley.

John was very good at French as I was. He was a year older than most of us, and had started his time at the school in the year before it moved from the old building at Crittalls Corner. In his first term there he had contracted a bad bout of mumps that had incapacitated him for most of the rest of that year. His Mother made an appeal to Pedley to let John do the first year again due to the time he had lost. Unburdened as he was by any trace of empathy in his being, Pedley of course refused to allow him to "resit" the year. John's Ma then appealed to the School Board and eventually his decision was overruled.

But spiteful men like Pedley had long memories. So when John bunked off school early after O levels Pedley sent the School Board round to formally investigate why John was not there. Interestingly they were never sent to see the two boys he had bunked off with – John Patching and Pete Staples

Patching was never going to come back anyhow – but Pete Staples was in the Sixth form in my class. So whereas bombing outrages were kept in house if the boys in question had Oxbridge potential, boys whose parents had dared to cross him were expelled for minor offences 5 years later. What an insecure and spiteful man he really must have been.

Anyhow John remained a member of the Orpington crowd, and in 1965 married Josie. I met Jenny my wife in 1966 and when she had met John a few times she could not decide which of us was the more bolshy. He and I used to argue the pitch and toss of just about everything: politics mostly. Especially during the extended games of cards that were often held at his house in Crockenhill into the wee small hours – sustained by not so wee drams.

After we got married we lost touch with John. He tracked me down on Facebook after 40 years and invited us to to his place in Anglesey. We now E Mail each other regularly. He has been a very enthusiastic contributor to this book – and not JUST because of our shared hatred of our late and unlamented Headmaster.

Entente cordiale

Gerard Delacroix was my pen pal So in the summer break I went to France on an exchange visit. His Father had a "Quincaillerie" - loosely, an Ironmongers shop – in the Latin Quarter of the City a few streets across from Boulevard St Michel. His Father represented the archetypal French "*petit bourgeois*". I remember him as a short stocky man, in dark blue dungarees, a beret stuck at an angle on his head and a Gitane hanging from his bottom lip. He and his wife were immensely kind and hospitable towards me during my stay in their apartment in the Marais. We revisited all the tourist sites I had been to the previous year – and went up the Eiffel Tower.

After a couple of days we took a train out of the City to Fontainebleau. Gerard's Grandmother owned a small Hotel outside the town in the Forest area close to Barbizon, famed as the eponymous home of the School of Painters headed by Rousseau (Theodor) and Jean Francois Millet. It remains to this day a leading centre for artists. I had a grand time in the Forest area. They had red squirrels then. Gerard's Grandmother was very grand – very *"ancien régime"*. A Widow, she always wore a starched white blouse with a frilled collar buttoned to the neck, dark ankle length skirts, a ram rod straight back, white hair swept back in a bun, no cosmetic - she was quite imposing.

I learnt many things about French domestic life that summer. I learned that the French do not have kettles – they did not drink tea and coffee was made in *cafetières*. They did not have 3 piece suites as the centre of the family home was the kitchen. I also learned the terrible truth on why France is the World Capital of Perfumes and *Eaux de Toilette*. The French have a natural aversion to bathing. They would much prefer to use perfume or talc than to use soap. On every part of the body. This applied to both sexes. Oh yes! It was not for nothing that Napoleon had once sent a message to Josephine after one of his many battles to tell her he would be back in Paris in 10 days time – and to make sure she did not wash in the meantime.

Dinnertime was also a surprise – Madame Delacroix served food in the now long gone peasant tradition. A typical meal might be *patè*, followed by *côtelets* with *frites*, accompanied by those uniquely French *petit pois* that are like tiny ball bearings to look at but are actually sweet when you come to eat them. *Paté* just never tastes the same outside of France. I think it is the higher garlic and salt content. Madame Delacroix would serve every course on the same plate – one constituent at a time. So after the *paté* you would get the meat – then after that was gone the *frites* and so on. Confusing until you got used to it – you never knew when you were finished. But it certainly saves on the washing up!.

Dessert did come on a separate plate. The French *patissier* is a master of his art. *Hôtesses* in France are judged by the quality of their *patissier.* In every home you get fantastic deserts. I did.

Gerard and I either spent our days at the Lido, where I perfected the "bomb" from the diving board, and we chatted up the girls. Or we would have coffee and beer at tables set outside on the pavement in front of a myriad of Cafés and Brasseries. On the wall of every hostelry there always two signs. One was the "Do not spit" sign I was accustomed to from the Metro the year before, the other read *"Repression de l'ivresse publique"* - Control of Public Drunkenness. Right. We explored the forest, hiking along the sun dappled pathways, and visited Barbizon several times. There was also a Fairground in town – the French proved to be equally as mad drivers on the dodgems as they were on the roads. We bought *"barbe a papa"* and *"bonbons"* from the sweets stand, shot at targets with air rifles. For the life of me I could not find a coconut shy or a hoopla.

My stay in Fontainebleau was the height of my year. Marred only by one unfortunate incident. I had met this vaguely Middle Eastern looking chap of around my own age when I went to the Lido on my own, and decided to take him back to Madame's house to offer him tea. Madame was icily polite, extremely formal - and very offhand.

Only after my new found "friend" had gone did Gerard tell me that he had in fact been an Algerian – and although De Gaulle had in fact granted Algeria independence earlier that very year, the Civil War of the 1950s had left the French with a very real hatred of his compatriots. Who until recently had been committing terrorist acts across France. *Oops* – a diplomatic incident.

The centre piece of the town of Fontainebleau is its magnificent Château. Dating originally from the 16th century when it had been a hunting lodge for Francis 1, it had been added to by successive Kings of France over the centuries. During the Second Empire in the 19th century Emperor Napoleon 111 had lavished money on it to provide a fitting Imperial home for him and his Empress Eugenie in place of the – now empty – Palais de Versailles. With over 1500 rooms, many stuffed with precious works of art, and set in 130 hectares of land, it had at that time the distinction of being the only Château in France to have been continuously inhabited for over 400 years.

In 1959 France was still in NATO, and it was occupied by SHAFE, Supreme Headquarters Allied Forces Europe.

(2013: *At this point I feel compelled to mention the decision this year by a "Child Protection Officer" of a local Council here in Britain to ban future student exchange visits between families in Europe on the basis that some children could witness domestic violence – or even suffer child abuse - in the family concerned!!! In future the children must stay in communal halls.*

I suppose with her job title she has to justify her existence somehow – as do so many of these over paid jobsworths – but this surely plumbs new depths of politically correct nannying? Apart from being the grossest of insults not just to the receiving families but also to the professionalism of the schools organising the exchanges. Does she really think that families with teenage children who allow their offspring to visit and to receive other kids are going to be child molesters in disguise? Or to be so dysfunctional as to resort to domestic violence in the presence of such children - or indeed at all?

This terminally deluded woman clearly has no real experience of life or of human interaction. Maybe the nature of her title has turned her mind and she sees abusers everywhere.? Does she have any historical examples of such things occurring? I will wager not. I on the other hand well remember the tragic events in France a decade ago now where a teenage school group of British kids from Kent were billeted together in exactly the same type of "safe" accommodation our demented friend is advocating. One night a local man broke in, kidnapped a young English girl and murdered her. He had known where to find her!! So much for Nanny's advice then.

Unless we rid ourselves of the yoke of the Nanny state, which strives constantly to dictate how we live our perfectly legal lives, then soon the last vestige of independent thought and self reliance will have been sucked out of we British. Then God help us – we shall become a bunch of neutered sheep unable to compete with just about any other nation.)

*

In September 1959 most of us in UVM were promoted to the School Premier League. No more History, Geography,Maths (hurrah) English or Science subjects. Just French, Spanish (from scratch in 2 years to A level, and German in 4+ yrs) Many of my classmates from the previous two years had come up with me. There was one notable newcomer – Pete Staples of Lower 5G and the Rugby Ist XV. Many of us were almost as surprised to see him join us as he himself must have been. He had got the right number and level of passes at O Level so was there on merit.

He hardly conformed to the classic profile for an academically minded lad, nor to the somewhat pious nature of some of the Class – notably but not exclusively Perriman, Priestley and Leeding., known to many of us as the three Bishops. I could at the time quite see one or all of them in cassocks sharing the Ecclesiastical Benches in the House of Lords. There was Terry

Smith, known rather sarcastically by some – and by me - as "Terence the Omniscient". (Nobody likes a know-all.) Another pet hate of mine was Westwood, a bumptious and self opinion-ated lad always laying the law down to somebody about something or other. (Rumour has it that he eventually became the Mayor of either Margate or Ramsgate in Kent. Either way, I can just imagine him in his finery, his Gold chain of Office around his neck, presiding over Council Meetings and opening libraries. It would have been the ideal role for someone as pompous and self-important as he was even at 16 years of age). Lastly, there were two boys named Simmonds – not related as I recall. Simmonds 1 was a poor spin bowler, but the other had an unfortunate behavioural tic. Every time a Master interro-gated the class in an attempt to uncover a miscreant for some infringement or another Simmonds 2 would blush furiously – and so often got punished for things he had never done. (*Not that we exploited this of course – heavens no!*)

The Course Work lay a heavy preponderance on Literature - at the expense of "*l' argot français*" actually employed by the French themselves. This showed itself to be the case in my very first essay in French in the 6ᵗʰ form. The good people of Fontainebleau call themselves "*les Bellifontaines*" The main market in the town has that name. Many towns in France have their own descriptive adjective – everyone else from outside understands them. The word is to be found in the 4 volume set of Larousse. It had never reached Carmarthenshire however. Three times I used it to describe my holiday in Fontainebleau in the summer. 3 times Taffy Jenkins crossed it out. He would hear none of it. It was not a word.

The French poets we had to study were Alfred de Musset, Alfred de Vigny, Theophile Gautier. Heard of any of them? No. There was no Verlaine, no Rimbaud – no internationally acclaimed poet at all. Except for dear old Victor Hugo. Deemed to be the most famous poet in France, although his poetry outside France was largely unknown. He may have become a member of the *Academie Française*, the French Institution that protects the purity of the language to this day, at the tender age of 40 - but by thunder could he rabbit on!!

I am reminded of the famous Spike Milligan description of Hitler's artistic prowess: "Hitler, there was a painter – a whole room, two coats in one afternoon" Substitute the words "Victor Hugo", "Poet", "1,000 lines of iambic pentameter" as appropriate and you get the gist. Tendentious, long winded – and so so boring.

He won more success and international acclaim with his two major novels, *Notre Dame de Paris,* better known to us as "The Hunchback of Notre Dame" and "Les Miserables", fondly referred to in our household as "The Glums". There was a much better set of reading matter - La Fontaine, the French Aesop, Guy de Maupassant, with his earthy tales of the Parisian demi monde. Last but far from least was *"Le Grand Meaulnes"* by Alain Fournier, for me one of the greatest first novels of the romantic genre ever written.

In fact his only novel, as he was killed in action in 1914 aged just 28. The book is a tale of a fruitless search for a lost love set in part against a wintry landscape that increases the sense of desolation. The book has twice been filmed, but you will be hard pressed to find it in any English bookshop as it was translated under several different titles.

Last on the list was "Le Cid" by Corneille. The dramatisation of the story of the Spanish nobleman who drove a Moorish Fleet from Spain. Immortalised by Charlton Heston in the eponymous Hollywood epic "El Cid".

For Spanish there was passion all the way. First *"La sirena negra"* - The Black Mermaid - by the 19th century Galician author Emilia Bazan – a story of temptation and lust. Then there was *"Pensativa"* the award winning novel of 1947 by the Mexican author Jesus Goytortua, set immediately after the Mexican revolution, telling the story of the hardships and cruelties witnessed and suffered by the eponymous heroine. One word more than any other will for me always typify this book – the Spanish adjective *"desnarigado"*. Literally it means "left with no nostrils" and describes a man who has had his nose cut off.

Then there was "Mariana Pineda" the dramatic masterpiece by Federico Garcia Lorca. It premiered in Barcelona in 1927 with stage sets designed by Salvador Dali. It was an allegory on Fascist extremism. Lorca was murdered in Granada at the beginning of the Spanish Civil War in August 1936 by Franquista forces. His body has never been found.

Jack Burnip took us for Spanish. A level Spanish in 2 years from scratch had always been a bit of a stretch. Spanish is a fairly straightforward Latin root language to learn – once you have learned the 450 irregular verbs. Yes, 450!! In four tenses – plus present and past subjunctives. It was, though, an excellent grounding for when we lived in Madrid at the turn of the 70s into the 80s.

German set books were frankly pretty pedestrian. No Goethe, no Schiller, no Heinrich Heine, no Rainer Maria Rilke or Thomas Mann. There was "Bahnwärter Thiel" by Gerhardt Hauptmann (?) about a pious railway signalman with a passionate wife who seeks excitement elsewhere. Then there was *"Der Prinz von Homburg"* by Heinrich von Kleist – what WAS all the fuss about? And then there was ""*Die schwarze Spinne*" or the Black Spider by the Swiss author Jeremias Gotthelf An allegory on the Plague in a Swiss village, a pact with the Devil to keep it out: – Gotthelf - God help us!

We boys of Lower V1 Modern spent the Autumn term of 1959 beginning to familiarise ourselves with these set books.

Colin

It had been around this time that I got back in touch with my old mate Colin. He and I had known each other since we had both attended St Nicholas at the age of 4. Strange to say "got back in with" when we had both been at the same school for the past 5 years. But that was just the way things went in a school with over 700 boys. Horizons broadened. Colin's Father had been an Army Officer in the War, and was very strict. He and Colin clearly had a bit of a stormy relationship – Fathers and sons thing. He would often ground him for long periods. He was also always on at him about doing well at school.

We both went to Chis and Sid where as I say for some reason we hardly saw each other for four years except in passing. By his own admission Colin was not really interested in academic matters – which did not exactly improve his relationship with his Dad. He landed in Lower 5G. He did not go up to the Sixth Form. All Colin wanted to do was go to Art School!

Colin was short like his Father and grew a beard when he got into his late teens – probably just to piss off Pater. I recently saw a photo taken at a party Colin threw when he was around 18. The girls in it are all dressed exactly like Cilla Black in her heyday in the early 60s. Colin on the other hand strongly resembles a larger version of "Grumpy" from the Seven Dwarfs with attitude. There goes my invite to the Villa in Portugal!

Anyhow in Christmas Week 1959 Colin's Father held a cocktail party and invited us all round. As I recall there was myself, Graham, Colin, Brains and a couple of his other mates whose names I forget. We all turned up in our sports jackets with our cravats – oh how cravats were popular around that time. The fashionable young man would have at least half a dozen in different colours and patterns. You fitted them with a long pin: leading to *One up Pin-manship* being the craze.

It was at this party that Colin's Father poured me my very first Whisky and Ginger Ale. What better memory than that can you have of a man?! (Colin eventually achieved his goal of becoming an artist. He went to the Royal Academy to study sculpture, and is now a sculptor of international repute working from his studio in his villa near Faro in Portugal.)

On New Years Eve 1959 you could almost hear the national sigh of relief that the 50s were over. At their outset Britain had still had the largest Empire the World has ever seen. The decade had also started with Britain deeply mired in austerity and had ended in growing prosperity. More houses were built in the 1950's than at any time before or since.

In 1950 the poor put upon housewife had had almost no household aids other than a Clothes Boiler, Mangle and Refrigerator. It is estimated that at that time she had worked 75 hours a week cooking and cleaning. By 1959 she had a whole range of new fitted kitchen options, new exciting materials such as Formica (**well it was then!**) and bright new paint colours, as well as a wealth of electric appliances; from ovens through food mixers to pressure cookers and Hoovers, hair dryers and coffee makers.

It has also been mooted that the bright colours of the modern man-made fabrics coming on to the market towards the end of the decade had been a key contributory factor to the creation of the modern day teenager.: that, and the invention of the transistor radio. In the Swinging Sixties, this would lead to teenagers replacing adults as the leaders of the Consumer Society.

By 1959 the Empire had already begun to slip from our grasp, and within a decade it would have become largely symbolic. But the 1960s still dawned with a great sense of optimism.

1960

This optimism must have spread across the Globe – it had certainly reached Hollywood. There were a whole string of new releases. "Psycho" with Anthony Perkins and Janet Leigh won Best Picture; whereas Burt Lancaster won Best Actor for "Elmer Gantry". How about these for a list of also rans? The second highest grossing film was Disney's "Swiss Family Robinson" with John Mills and Dorothy MacGuire as the parents. "Spartacus" with Kirk Douglas, "The Apartment" with Jack Lemmon and Shirley Maclaine and "Oceans 11" with the Rat Pack of Sinatra, Martin, Lawford and Sammy Davis Junior were snapping at their heels. Last but far from least is one of my own Top 10 favourite movies, "The Alamo" with John Wayne as Davy Crockett and Laurence Harvey as Colonel Jim Bowie. A film that in itself has quite simply become part of American folklore.

I was approaching 17, and like all young men my fancy had turned to having a good time as often as possible. The Orpington crowd as we came to be known was growing in number all the time. There were now perhaps 8 – 10 regulars: Colin, John Sachs, Graham Mochrie, Johnny Baker, Johnny Vowles, Howard Wilkinson, Harry Pattullo. One other member of the group was a childhood friend of Graham and Howard, with whom in later life I have become close. He does not want his name mentioned in this book, so I have dubbed him "Brains". We only saw him in the holidays as he was up at Selwyn College Cambridge for 3 years.

Sadly John Sachs and Johnny Vowles are no longer with us. As for the rest of the above named, I lost touch with them all for more than 40 years – until John Baker tracked me down on Facebook, and then Graham, who had been my Best Man at our wedding, rang my brother from Toronto in 2007, after not being able to find my Ex Directory number, to ask him where we had been since 1978. Since that time we have met with Graham and Caroline and Howard and Maureen in Antibes and Toronto, with "Brains" and his wife Tove in Antibes and in Devon and Harry in Orpington. I have spent a weekend with Johnny Baker and Josie on their farm in North Wales. I am still getting round to Colin and Mort.

The reunions have needed careful planning. This is because of what I call the Great Orpington Diaspora. Only Johnny Baker and Harry are in the UK. Graham emigrated to Toronto with his family in 1978. Howard went to the US in the early 1960s and now lives in California. Colin is now an internationally recognised sculptor – lives on the Algarve in Portugal. "Brains" married a Danish girl and has lived in Denmark for 40 years.

Whatever else there may or may not be, we all of us have one thing in common as children of the 1940's. We are each still married after more than 40 years to the same girl. 280 years of married life. That must be something of a record these days. I wonder how many groups of married men in their 20s today will still be able to say that in 40 years time.

Friday and Saturday nights were our time. You could always perm at least four from ten or so of us at any given moment. We prided ourselves as a group on having attended some form of party almost every weekend – without ever having been invited. Yes this was gatecrashing, but the parties were largely amongst our much wider group of middle class teenage contemporaries. We were all a pretty civilised bunch. Our view was that we added class to the proceedings (*yeah, right!*) We chatted / picked up girls, got gently rat-arsed and did no damage. (There may have been one or two exceptions to this. I couldn't possibly comment – absolutely not.)

I just know that I am going to get a barrel load of his legendary sarcastic remarks for writing this, but Graham is maybe the soundest most straightforward and most level headed of all the friends I have been fortunate to have made over the years. I would hazard a guess that part of the reason for this was that his Father sadly died very young. Long before I first knew him. And partly because he has Scottish blood in him. Although his Mother was of Italian extraction.

He was a Public schoolboy, attending Dulwich College as a day boy. Where he tells me that he was not always a saint. I cannot recall when I first met him – maybe through Colin who was part of the Petts Wood crowd. One day he was not there, then he was. I now consider him to be my best friend. He was my Best Man at our wedding. For several years he knocked about with Sheila, a tall blonde girl. Everyone thought they might get hitched. Then it ended – no idea why. A few years later he married Caroline, who was the antithesis of Sheila - a short dark haired "petite gamine" of a girl. Like the rest of us, they are still together after more than 40 years. Everyone loves Caroline.

Graham became a metallurgist and worked for Rolls Royce in Derby. They had a black cat he called Mog – see what I mean about straightforward – and my wife took one of the first of her kittens and developed a whole new dynasty at our cottage in Sussex. Then they went out to Kitwe in Zambia to work in the Mining Industry. Came back to Camborne, then emigrated to Toronto in 1978. We lost track of each other for over 30years.

Like the rest of us though Graham had his moments in his teens. Like for instance when he and Colin had catapult fights on the deserted former WW11 Anti - Aircraft Gun site outside Petts Wood. Or when they made and let off pipe bombs on the same ground. Colin "cooked" his own Devil's brew of Sodium Chlorate weed killer and Sugar in a shed at home. Apparently even the fumes from the mixture could take your eyebrows off! A *Jetex* fuse of the kind used in model aircraft was stuffed into the end of the finished article then lit – and bang! Good – but highly dangerous - fun was had by all (*Do not try this at home – or at all! Ever. You could lose a limb – or become a star attraction for the Security Services: or both*)

Why then do I consider this bomb making good for a laugh yet at the same time condemn Walker & Co for letting off bombs at school? It is certainly true that both deeds were pretty stupid and highly dangerous. But it is one thing for two young men to let off bombs in a deserted area when both are in on the act and aware of what is going on. It is quite another to let off bombs covertly and indiscriminately and without any warning on or close to school grounds where up to 700 boys could be running around.

Poverest Woods was another haunt of ours. You had to avoid the Poverest Boys from the local Council Estate. (They roamed that part of town, the Homefield Rise mob had the territory in the town centre and up Spur Road.) Both gangs were always looking for trouble. It got so bad at one point that Colin started taking a borrowed air rifle with him when we went up there. This back-fired badly one day when he fired off a pellet at random – and shot David Moss instead. The poor fellow was laid flat out on the ground, a pellet sticking out of his forehead between and just above the eyes. He quickly came round – and as Colin later related so did the police and David's parents. We did not see Colin for a while – he was grounded. Excellent shooting though.!

Mrs B's Finishing School for Boys

Our experiences round at Mrs B's house represented such a uniquely unusual state of affairs that I still sometimes wonder if it wasn't all a dream. On weekday nights Johnny Sachs and I would often drop round to Mrs B, who lived in Hill View Road. Where we would often find others of our number already there, sitting at the kitchen table, smoking, drinking and playing cards. Smoking was practically a condition of entry. Mrs B chain smoked Craven A. Must have been on at least 60 a day. It was a unique social milieu – a middle aged, middle class lady running a kind of social club for teenagers in her own home.

I feel sure that today in our Nanny State the Social Services would be sniffing round just on the basis of hearing about it, invoking Child Protection laws. Maybe even the Police would be around making enquiries. The tabloids would whip themselves into a frenzy!

There would have been absolutely no need. One of the main reasons for the Mrs B's "Social Club" was her daughter Patty, a blonde pocket Venus who was - let us say - a very popular girl. Boyfriends a plenty were always crossing the threshold. Another spin off reason was probably that Mrs B just treasured the company. Her husband was a Marine Surveyor for Lloyds Register of Shipping, and was always travelling the globe. I think he was actually at home only once in all the many times I was there.

Our hostess introduced us to Mah Jong, Canasta - and various types of exotic booze. It was a bit like a finishing school for boys. I remember that on one occasion she even produced a bottle of Polish Vodka with gold leaf inside. Visits to her house were always something to look forward to. Especially when Penny "persuaded" us – as if! - to play strip poker. I shall draw a veil over the rest – which, happily, she never did.

The only time I recall that sexual harassment ever did rear its head at Mrs B's was one evening a week before Christmas one year when mistletoe was up in the hallway. As John and I arrived one of Mrs B's friends who had been visiting, a lady of ample proportions and a certain age, no doubt flushed with a couple of G&Ts, grabbed John and planted a big wet kiss on his lips. John took it bravely. One of the drawbacks of being a bit of a lady's man I guess.

※

Other haunts of our crowd for the next few years would largely feature licensed premises. The Anchor and Hope in the High Street - which I noticed recently is now a Noodle Bar – springs immediately to mind. I used to pop in there once or twice a week when I was 17, along with whichever of the crowd was about. I will always remember when I went in there on the day of my 18th birthday, having been a regular for some months – and got slung out as under age by the new Barman! Another port of call was the Artichoke, now also sadly no more. The highlights of the Saloon Bar here were always the vociferous but friendly religious arguments between the Vicar of All Saints and his Catholic counterpart from Holy Innocents.

The Vicar drank Brown and Mild if I remember – the Priest always drank Guinness. He spoke with a broad Irish brogue. They would often argue – and drink – for most of the evening. They always parted friends, sometimes with one supporting the other down the road. They were a variety act. *Now that is what I call Ecumenicalism.: "Never mind the Synod boys and girls – everyone down the pub!"*

※

Brown and Mild? What we drank then was different. Until the mid 60s the Beer Drinkers' favourite tipple was Mild Ale. This would often be mixed with bottled Stout (but not Guinness) or a bottle of Brown Ale to give a pint of Stout and Mild or Brown and Mild. (If you had a Mackeson's Cream stout with it, the drink almost tasted a bit sweet.) This truly was food in a glass. A malty flavour, full of calories, 3.6% alcohol. Bitter came a poor second. There was no draught lager – except Harp Lager from Guinness if you called that a beer. It wasn't. It was called several other things mind. Yet sadly, for reasons nobody has ever really understood, people just stopped drinking Mild from the mid 60s onwards, and it is almost impossible to find it any more.

Some even stranger drinks could be on the menu. During the spring of 1960 I clearly recall a rumour that began to circulate that one of the boys in our year, David Ross, somewhat of an athlete, had developed an addiction for one unusual form of tipple – Cough Linctus. I have no way of knowing if this was true – but why make it up? Several classmates swore to all who would listen that they had seen David polish off an entire bottle in one swig. The price of a pint in 1960 was around one shilling and three pence (6.25p). *Far less per pint than cough linctus!*

Maybe I am doing the guy a gross disservice. Many of the cough medicines at that time contained opiates. They therefore were quite effective pain killers. David trained hard as an athlete, and may have suffered pain as a result.

Addiction to hard drugs was in any case unknown in Britain in our formative years. Believe it or believe it not, but until well into the 1950s heroin had been widely prescribed by Doctors as a pain killer! The addictive nature of the drug had still not been recognised. In June 1955 the "Times" had written a Leader quoting Health Service figures showing that there were just 317 registered drug addicts in the nation. Of these just 15% were heroin addicts – giving the grand total of just 47.5 heroin addicts in total. Registered addicts could get prescriptions for the drug from their Doctor. I seem to recall from the early Sixties that a Late Night Chemist in the West End of London became notorious as a meeting point for addicts.

Yes - life was so different then.

*

Back at the Pub, the only diversions were the dartboard, the shove halfpenny table and maybe if you were lucky a Bar Billiards table. Television – no way. Pubs were for drinking, social mixing and for convivial conversation. But Pubs were not open 24/7 like they are now. In Wales they did not open at all on a Sunday. Some Welsh Parishes were still "dry" 24/7. In England they opened 10.00AM till 2.30PM, and 6.00 to 10.30PM So conviviality had to be continued elsewhere

Then, in late 1959 Di Vito's Coffee Bar had opened in the High Street. It had booths not tables, bench seats not chairs. *Trés avant garde* in 1960, believe me. What was even more *avant garde* was that some of us wore jeans. These new "American trousers" were still frowned upon by many parents of the day as being "too common and signifying a rebellious nature"!!

Jock de Vito was a Glaswegian of Italian descent. He was a very short stocky man with extremely hairy arms – he was also a dead ringer for Danny di Vito the Hollywood Film star. Only the broad Scottish accent gave him away. He ran the place like a martinet, treating his staff, managed by his son, and his customers – us and our kind – with equal disdain.

Jock may have been short, but we saw him more than once physically eject young men much taller and larger than himself from the premises. That was clearly the Glaswegian in him.

We would always meet up in Di Vitos on a Saturday morning to plan which parties were happening that night based on the various options identified by local rumour or actual known fact. We could make a coffee last a long while while we ogled the girls at the next table.

Vino

Talking of those of Italian descent brings me on to wine – or the lack of it – in our party years. Nowadays the British are some of the more enthusiastic and knowledgeable of wine aficionados. The British Supermarket chains have put most of the specialist Wine shops – my beloved Oddbins being a prime example – out of business by undercutting them on price. But at least the Supermarkets do now sell a broad range of decent enough wines from all over the world.

They have never sold *"Hirondelle"*. Nor do they stock Red or White wine of uncertain and unmarked vintage in boxes from Stowells of Chelsea or Grants of St James; nor cheap Hock or *Piat Noir*. (However, Blue Nun *Liebfraumilch* has made a surprising comeback in recent years.) If you really wanted to show off to your friends then you bought *Mateus Rosé* (a decent enough wine if you like *rosé*) from Portugal. Its major selling point as far as I could see was the unique shape of the bottles it came in. They must have been turned into a million table lamps in Britain in the 1960s.

That was it – the sum total of wine options available at High Street Off Licences in 1960. It was not until package tours to Europe started in earnest in the mid 70s that people began to sample proper wine, and quickly came to realise what awful dross was being foisted on them by British Wine Merchants. The rest is history – cheers!

As well as Di Vitos, another port of call for socialising was the Orpington Wimpy Bar. They were the only Fast Food chain I remember from those days. I think it was about this time that the first Wimpy Bar came to Orpington. A Franchise Burger chain run by J Lyons, the Restaurant chain, the brand had been founded in the US in the 30s. Lyons had begun the British side of the business in 1950. Whereas MacDonalds' had Ronald McDonald, a clown, as a mascot Wimpy Bars were named after J Wellington Wimpy, the little fat man in the Popeye cartoons. For a while Wimpy was popular with us British youth: but then McDonalds began to dominate and in the end the Wimpy Bar Burger chain was finally sold to Burger King in the 80s.

I turned 17 in April. I spent several months learning to drive with Dad. He had ditched the Morris 10 in 1959 and bought a new car, the Ford Popular 100E four door saloon. This had cutting edge technology (for 1959), went round corners at above 30 mph without endangering lives, had a smooth ride with a proper exhaust system that did not leak fumes. I passed my test first time.

1960 had more than its fair share of momentous events. In February The Prime Minister Harold Macmillan made his famous "Wind of Change" speech in Cape Town, signalling the beginning of the end for colonialism.

In February Hugh Heffner opened the first Playboy Club, in Chicago.

In March many South African blacks were massacred by Police at the township of Sharpeville when they marched to protest against being forced to carry ID cards; unlike the white South Africans.

In April a Mr Tim Dinslade produced a photo that he alleged showed proof of the existence of "Nessie" – the monster that had always been said to inhabit Loch Ness in Scotland. Controversy has raged over this photo ever since.

In May Princess Margaret, sister of the Queen, married Anthony Armstrong-Jones, a Society photographer - and a commoner.

Then in August an infamous culinary event occurred – the opening of the first Motorway "Restaurant" in Britain, on the

M1 at Newport Pagnell. Thus was heralded in an ignoble era of truly atrocious fried and dried up food at ridiculously high prices that remains to this day.

Perhaps the most momentous event was in November that year in the US, when John F Kennedy was elected President.

Or maybe for us Brits it occurred on December 9th, when the very first episode of Coronation Street was screened on Television –?

Porno

It is time now that I must raise the subject of Pornography in the 1950s and early 60s. Don't get too outraged – or too excited. There was none. *Nada.* Not even "Glamour Mags". *Playboy magazine* did not appear until several years after they opened their first premises in Chicago in 1960. (It was promptly banned in Britain when it did) In 1960 every newspaper, magazine and Motion Picture for public distribution had by law to conform to the strict condition laid down by the Lord Chancellor's Office that "all published material had to be fit and proper for public consumption." They were the sole arbiter of what this was. (*Yes my friends – it was naked censorship!*)

This meant that there were no Page 3 girls (or indeed no Sun newspaper) in 1960. No adult mags on the top shelves of W H Smith, no soft porn movies with simulated sex. No TV programmes or movies with any nudity at all. In Hollywood the studios themselves had a strict rule that in any scene shot in a bedroom the couple had to remain fully clothed and the man had to keep one foot on the floor at all times – must have been pretty difficult for Mickey Rooney at 5ft 2!

This made it especially difficult for hormonal young lads such as myself to gain sight of the naked female form. You could buy "dirty" postcards from spivs on street corners in Soho. But even inside the clip joints there was no - LEGAL - nudity.

The – slightly – more respectable big Clubs such as the Windmill and Raymond's Revue Bar got around this by claiming that their girls were performing tableaux of historic events.

Eventually the Lord Chancellor's Office agreed to this – provided that the girls remained motionless and stony faced. (In the TV series "Budgie" in the 1970s its star Adam Faith plays a Soho fixer. At one club the doorman would chant to passers-by the immortal words "They are naked - and they move") The whole thing was absurd, but censorship like this continued until the end of the decade.

There were *samizdat* sex films from Europe that were always being seized in police raids. But for the average young man in Orpington there was no legal access to the female form in all its glory —except at the small shop further down the High Street on the right hand side past Chislehurst Road. Here you could buy – in a plain brown wrapper – the latest edition of "Health and Efficiency" Magazine. The official journal of the British Naturist Society.

The Publication had avoided Censorship by proving it was a serious publication providing health advice for British Nudists – as indeed it was. But I will wager good money that the majority of its "readers" were teenage boys such as myself.!

Yes, as I will keep telling you. The world was a very very different place in those days.

*

At Easter 1960 100,000 misguided supporters of CND - the Campaign for Nuclear Disarmament – had marched the 50 miles from London to the Atomic Weapons Research Establishment at Aldermaston in Berkshire in support of unilateral nuclear disarmament – aka surrendering the nation to rule from Moscow. Soon after the march the School Debating Society proposed the motion that CND had a just cause. It was rejected by a thumping two to one majority.

In the summer of 1960 two prefabricated classrooms appeared in the quad at the back of the school. First rumours were that this was to be a punishment block where Pedley could incarcerate those who had transgressed against his regime. We had visions of barbed wire and searchlights, and of tunnels being dug to reach the woodlands beyond the school field. Then the Huts were given the more prosaic names of Hut A and Hut B. They were there to house the ever growing population of the school, as the "baby boomers" of the post war years grew into teenagers. (In fact they would indeed have apparently made excellent punishment blocks – in summer the boys in them were baked by the heat, in winter they choked on the fumes of the oil stoves.)

At Easter Gerard Delacroix came to us for the return visit. It was the first time he had been to Britain and, frankly, he found it to be something of a culture shock. The pavement Café and *Brasserie* culture of France were almost the direct antithesis of the British pub. In the former you could sit outside in the sun and linger for hours over a coffee and a croissant that was brought to you with a smile and a friendly *"Bon jour"* (except in Paris). In the other you had to queue for your beer - which was brown! - and pay for it in advance. There was was nothing edible available. (Pickled eggs were the only delicacy to be found in pubs in those days – plus plain potato crisps with little wraps of blue paper containing salt inside the packet)

Mon dieu! You could not linger. Twice a day they threw you out and closed.!! He never really got his head around this. The food we served him at home was also a mystery. There were no *baguettes*, the staple food of France. What were these corn-flakes? Baked Beans? And how could you call these *saucisses*?

Tea was the only drink option – or chicory coffee extract. (*Ugh, what muck that was!*) He drank milk mostly.

To be frank Mum was not the greatest cook in the world – I guess almost 15 years of rationing had taken the edge off it for her. She did a great 90 second boiled egg, while at the same time giving the sprouts 30 minutes on a high gas! Her curried mince was – well, unforgettable to be kind. But she did cook a great steak and kidney pie, and her apple pie with fruit from the garden was truly historic - especially when served with hot Bird's Custard. We had a Roast most Sundays. It lasted 3/4 days depending on size. Cold meat on Mondays, Meat pie or rissoles on Tuesday, stew on Wednesdays. Gerard was a well brought up lad, so he bore all of these to him totally alien dishes with a brave face.

We spent our days in Di Vitos, where he could at least have an Espresso, or up in London doing the tourist spots. It was a good visit. But I felt that he must have breathed a sigh of relief when he got on the boat train in Victoria Station in London. I wish I had been a fly on the wall when he reported back to his countrymen - "*Les anglais, ce sont assez sympa – mais la cuisine, que c'est saugrenue!*"

Religion at school

One school subject I have failed to mention up until now is Religious Instruction We had studied this from the very first week at school. It had been a legal requirement. In the 50s and 60s the majority of the population still considered themselves to be practising Christians, and weekly Church attendances were in the high millions. I myself had been confirmed into the C of E. I had even been a choirboy at All Saints when I was about 8. (Happily no pictures exist!) The Church of England remained the bellwether of social mores – abortion was a mortal sin and a crime, as was homosexuality. Divorce was heavily frowned upon. Hell fire and damnation awaited the sinner. This was a time when the Church still wielded great power and influence. The Bishops in the House of Lords saw to that. They constituted a strong lobby for the righteous.

By the time we got to the 6th Form RI had become more of a philosophical discussion group – and therefore much more lively. Our moderator in discussions was Jack Burnip who had introduced the study of Comparative Religion – quite an avant garde approach in the Christian 1950s. I remember one such discussion on Buddhism in RI when Terry Smith – never someone to hide his light under a bushel – got to a point in his planned lecture where he modestly stated "Now even I had difficulty understanding this bit". With such arrogance he could only have ended up as a politician – although I have been watching every political story in the Press ever since and have not spotted his name.

In another similar philosophical exchange some-one – I forget who now, but Terry was always a serial offender so perhaps it was him again - was maintaining that there was a scientific explanation for life without a God. He then expounded an argument in which he posited that life was brought about by electrical impulses in the brain according to nature. I could contain myself no longer that day and heckled him with the question "OK that is how it happens, but why does it happen,?" He could not provide an answer.

Why - it is the great mystery that Science can never solve.

There was another Philosophy discussion group that I valued greatly that lay outside course work or curriculum. This was run by Cedric Morley, the Physics Master. In this group we examined basic laws of physics and discussed all aspects of their effect on our lives. He also covered the rudiments of Chemistry and Astronomy. We were shown some short films that I suppose had been made by the Central Office of Information detailing the horrors of nuclear war in cartoon form. I recall one where a missile is flying over sea and land on its way to its target. Quite chilling and thought provoking.

In retrospect I can see the purpose of these discussions – apart from giving Cedric the opportunity to chain smoke at the back of the class when the lights were down. Thought had been given by the school to the fact we were headed for University, and the broadening of our intellectual compass through sessions such as these would stand us in good stead.

In August we went on holiday, this time to Mudeford near Bournemouth. It was as usual a fairly quiet affair This was to be the very last time that I ever went on holiday with my family. The next four summers were going to be very different kettles of fish.

Home base

The centre of operations for the Orpington Crowd in 1960 - and for the following 3/4 years - was "The Maxwell" Public House. Strategically sited in Station Road just down from Station Approach, it stood just outside the town, making it ideal for reaching from Petts Wood, Crofton, Spur Road and Goddington and Tubbenden Lane. Our fame was spreading, and our ranks were swelling every day (well OK that may just be a *bit* of an exaggeration)

I think it was Harry who first introduced us to the place, as he lived in Tubbenden Lane then. It became the Head Office and Operations Centre for the unofficial Orpington Crowd. (We were all far too well brought up ever to be considered either a Gang or a Mob)

Mine host was known universally as "Skip" A tall, slim – almost thin – man with glasses and a ramrod straight back, he had a huge Bull Mastiff whose sole aim in life seemed to be to have just one more sausage. I never saw a dog eat like that one. Still, a well fed guard dog was always to be preferred – he looked like he could easily manage a whole burglar or a drunk. Skip always had a rather world weary expression coupled with a business like approach to everything. I guess he could have been a Warrant Officer in the War. But nobody but nobody ever talked about the war in those days. We certainly put a smile on his face, given what we spent in the Pub over the next 3 or so years.

It all happened at the Maxwell. There were always six or seven of us in there minimum in the Public Bar on a Friday night. In addition to the close mates already named, there might be John Chapman, Mick Butterly, Joe Swain, Alan Wall — the list goes on and on. Many pints were sunk, the dog always ponced something to nibble on. It was conviviality writ large. One of the highlights of the evening – or its nadir whichever way you looked at it – was Mick Butterly setting light to his own farts. A dramatic event to behold. Oh how we laughed.

Then there was Howard "Moby" Millbank. Like the rest of us he was strong willed with a mind of his own (It was almost a pre-condition of entry to the Orpington Crowd. Discussions as to what we might do the following weekend for example were a bit like a sitting of the Israeli Knesset – without the fisticuffs). This was perhaps best shown to be so in Moby's case when he got into an argument one evening with Brian Calver. Brian had been attempting to make his point over and again with no success.

Exasperated he finally said to Millbank "Every time I try to argue something with you Moby, all you say is" Bol—ks." Moby looked him straight in the eye – and said "Bo—ks!" One for the history books that.

The Maxwell had been in business a long time. So it had already amassed plenty of regulars before we came along. Our haunt was the Public Bar so some of the other drinkers were a bit on the rough side. One in particular a big burly bricklayer a bit older than us often used to get a bit pissed and start moaning about us taking over the place. One night he was sitting on a bench seat along one wall when Graham came in and went to sit next to him. At the last minute he noticed the bench was cracked with splintered wood, so went to sit somewhere else saying "I don't want to sit next to that crack"

Our burly friend growled menacingly. "Who are you calling crap?" It took us three minutes or so to convince him what Graham had actually said. It was a close run thing though. He was an awfully big fellow. So the Maxwell was not always nirvana for us.

There was one Sunday lunchtime at the Maxwell that I remember particularly well. Colin, Harry myself and a couple of the other guys were there as usual. Colin challenged Harry to a game of darts for half a crown. Harry won, so Colin said double or quits. 8 games later he owed Harry £32. A small fortune in 1960. Being like the rest of us resourceful, Colin then bravely challenged Harry to a game of 3 card brag – and by the end of the afternoon they were even again!

We often ended up in the Chinese Restaurant by the War Memorial at the end of the High Street after closing time on a Friday night. This once led to Joe Swain and Alan Wall gaining notoriety in the local Paper under the byline **"Meal cost them more"**. They had got a bit drunk one night in the pub (perfectly natural thing to do- that is why it was there) and after eating they decided they did not feel like paying. So they did a bunk through the window of the Gents. The first we knew of this was when several Chinamen armed with meat cleavers dashed through from the kitchen and out the main entrance. They

cornered the two further down the High Street, and – luckily
for them – called the Police. They were fined by the Local
Magistrates – and had to pay the Bill. Never a dull moment on
a Friday night!.

But it was the weekend we looked forward to the most.
Although I possessed a full Driving Licence by now, I was still
at school and could not afford a car. Dad was loath to lend me
his as I was a new driver. In any case he needed our's six days
a week to go to Park Langley. Because in those days everybody
worked a five and half day week. The Weekend started at
12.30pm on a Saturday for the working population. This is
why football – which then was so very much more a working
class game than today – had become so popular. The men
would stream out of the factories on Saturday lunchtime, and
straight into their local ground. A pie and a pint and a hard
fought match was what they yearned for the whole week long.
3.00PM kick off on a Saturday was the only time for football.
It would be another 30 years and more at least before the clubs
even got legal permission to play on a Sunday. The Lord's Day
Observance Society and the Bishops in the House of Lords saw
to that.

But all was not lost if we wanted to go to the coast on a
Saturday. There was a local Chauffeur Hire service in the High
Street at the junction with Broomhill Road. They had an interesting collection of old American Packards, complete with
running boards and white walled tyres. (The marque disappeared in 1958.) They also had a few Mark 1 Ford Populars for
self drive hire. Several of us would club together to hire one of
these, and then we would drive it down to Hastings or Brighton
on a Saturday morning. Harry, Graham, Johnny Vowles, sometimes Howard, Brains when he was down from Cambridge or
Colin – perm any three or four from seven. We would rattle
down the A21 through Sevenoaks, Tonbridge, Robertsbridge
and Battle to Hastings. Where we would then settle into our

home from home – The Anchor in George Street. (The time record for the trip according to Harry was when he went down with a mate of his in a souped -up Simca. The length of the A21 in just over the hour.)

I believe that our group may be the only bunch of drinkers who have ever drunk a pub dry of Worthington White Shield, a strong bottled Pale Ale no longer brewed. We achieved this feat one Saturday lunchtime in the Anchor. There is another humorous little anecdote of the times we all spent there. One day, well on the way to inebriation, we ordered hard boiled eggs from the barman. When they arrived Brains – who like the rest of us had had a few - became overcome with conviviality. In a display of his renowned intellectual capacity he said "I know how I'll get the shell off" - and cracked it over my head. Doubtless this was a trick they played on you at High Table in Cambridge! At this very moment the barman appeared at the table with a salt cellar in his hand, and asked if we wanted salt with our eggs. Several of the assembled company fell off their chairs laughing.

There was more laughter in the Bar during one trip to Hastings in October 1960. We were in the Anchor as usual when a bunch of lads from South London came in. Chattering like a flock of sparrows one of them suddenly said in a loud voice "Did you hear about poor old Frankie? He was attending a public gathering when the floor collapsed!!" The rest of them roared with laughter and they went back to their drinks.

Gallows humour – a British speciality. The Frankie in question had been Francis Forsyth. He had been hanged for murder in Wandsworth Prison the week before. He was 18 yrs old. He had been a member of a gang of four youths who had kicked another youth to death in a robbery. One other member of the gang was hanged with him. The punishment still fitted the crime in 1960 – although capital punishment was finally abolished in Britain in 1969.

As for driving back home from forays to the seaside, the simple truth was that we often drove when we were well over the limit – or would have been had there been one. There were no breathalysers in 1960. The only test the Police applied to assess if you were fit to drive was to see if you could balance on one leg, touch your nose with your eyes closed, walk along a straight line or repeat some tongue twister such as the apocryphal "The Leith Police dismisseth us" or "Peter piper picked a peck of pickled peppers". Just as well old Milton was not on the force – he would have had them doing forward rolls in a straight line!!!.

Normally the Rozzers only pulled you over if you were driving dangerously. In 1960, there were still only a few million licensed vehicles of all types on the road, so if you swerved around a bit there was a very good chance you would not hit anything – except maybe a lamp post.

Oh yes driving could be pretty hairy in 1960. And much more fun!

*

Over the next couple of years Johnny Sachs, Johnny Vowles and Howard all got cars of their own. Johnny Sachs had an old pre war Morris 8 – which spent a lot of time in the workshop. Johnny Vowles had an old Morris if I remember correctly. One of the abiding memories I will always have of "Johnny V" is of him driving up Poll Hill on the A21 between Sevenoaks and home with his head out of the sun roof - and each of us taking turns to stand with him.!!

As for Howard, he had an old Jowett 8 which he somehow managed to roll over in Petts Wood one sunny afternoon. Soon afterwards he emigrated to North America and has been there ever since. Unrelated events he insists. Oh happy days.

This was not the first car Howard had possessed. Although the first one never left his driveway. At that time there had been an orchard at the bottom of Scads Hill near to the Surgery of our GP Doctor Scales. There was a fruit stall near the entrance and the owner was selling a 1935 Austin 7 tourer. Howard tells me that his Dad bought it for him – for £3. He tried to repair it with parts from Pride and Clark in Brixton, but it proved too much of a task. In the end Howard's Dad gave it to the rag and bone man when he came round with his horse and cart. The car weighed not very much so he tried to tow it behind his cart. But the steering was completely shot, so in the end he had to cut it up section by section with a hacksaw and came back several times to take all of it away.

Howard went to Chis and Sid with me. Although I do not really remember him there. He had grown up with Graham and Brains, and was not one of my closest mates at the time. As promised – and with his permission - I detail below in his own words how he came to be a choirboy at the Coronation in 1953.

"My father was a coal miner from a coal mining family in County Durham. He and three of his four brothers would walk three miles out under the North Sea each day to start with their hacking and hewing. (they didn't start to get paid until they reached the coal face.)

His brothers loved it, my dad hated it and he used his fine alto singing voice to get a job as a poorly paid "Lay Singer" at Winchester Cathedral. From there he went to Durham then to St Pauls and finally to Southwark. He became pretty well known in the rarefied community of Ecclesiastical Singing. This allowed my brother Mike to try out for and be accepted into the Chapel Royal St. James' Palace choir.

Four years later I did the same and in April 1953 I joined the choir, just in time for the Coronation in June. Many choirs in

Britain sent two choristers to the Coronation, except the Abbey choir and our choir who sang in full complement, men and boys. We were the Queen's "personal choir". They gave us both medals for that. It was quite an intimidating experience for a 9 yr old

We received a scholarship to the City of London School which allowed us to get to choir practice at St James Palace four nights a week. I quit in 1956 and with my 11+ in hand transferred to Chis and Sid"

Howard's brother Mike went on to become a stellar success as an entrepreneur in the US Steel Industry, In the 1980s he took over Kaiser Steel for a time. Howard worked with him for a while then moved to California and ran his own business there. They recently got back together on a new joint venture. You could not want much more of a rags to riches story than that. From the coal mines of County Durham to the peak of the US Steel business in just one generation.

Johnny Vowles was a tall, rangy lad with bright ginger hair. He was at Dulwich College with Graham. Like the rest of us, he was a bit of a rebel - and a demon driver. John was always a bit gung ho and often got into scrapes. He and I were up in the West End of London one Saturday evening when we came across two drunks having a fist fight in the street. One was much smaller than the other – so John jumped in to break it up. The sight of this tall gangly slightly mad looking red haired bloke with those bulging eyes wading in caused the larger guy to stagger off. Typical JV moment!

Another story about JV was told me by Howard. Sometime in the early 1960s the Police announced a firearms amnesty. Just hand them in no questions asked. One evening Howard and John were driving around the area. Howard stopped outside the local nick. John jumped out of the car clutching according to Howard a large handgun and what appeared to be a rifle. He rushed into the Police station, slammed the guns on to the counter, yelled "Amnesty" at the top of his voice and rushed out again. Howard did a racing start – not easy in his old Jowett! Another true JV moment indeed. *(This was several years before John joined the Army. I can only assume that he had "lifted" them from the armoury at Dulwich College.)*

Anyhow he married June, an Anglo- Indian girl in 1966 and they had two sons, Warren and Peter.

For several years after that John and I served together in the same specialist Army Unit – one where my German skills would prove of great value. He then became part of the Greater Orpington diaspora, first working in Lebanon then moving his family to the New World where we all lost touch with him.

Graham tracked his sister down in the UK about 2 years ago now. She told him that John's elder son Warren had drowned years before whilst swimming in a lake somewhere in America. John had never really recovered from this tragedy. He and June got divorced. He fell on hard times, and had been living in relative poverty for a long time before he suffered a series of strokes in 2009/10 and sadly passed away in New Hampshire in December 2010.

John was a good friend to all of us and made a valuable personal contribution to our struggle against the Soviets in the Cold War. He attained the rank of Captain in the Intelligence Corps. He did not deserve to suffer the vicissitudes of life that he did. Man proposes, God disposes. Amen.

*

Sometimes at weekends we could not afford the car hire, so we hitch hiked. This was a common practice in those days. The best way was to go with a girl. She would hitch and when there was a taker the chaps would appear from out of the bushes and get a lift as well. Probably. Harry and I several times hitched down to Brighton with Patty B. They all stopped for her.

When we were in Brighton we always dropped by the "King and Queen" Pub just down from the Old Steyne. This was a large echoing Bar lined with barrels. There was also a large room where they often had folk music. I understand that the "King and Queen" is still very much in business today. Hooray!

One of the main drawbacks of hitching to the seaside was the trip back. This tended to be a solo affair as we tended to leave at different times. Often determined by our state of personal inebriation. The return trip was often on a Sunday morning after we had slept it off on the beach. *The coldest I have ever felt in my life was one Easter Sunday when I awoke in just a T shirt and shorts under an overturned dinghy on the sands. Chilled to the bone does not begin to describe it.*

As it was a Sunday, traffic was almost non – existent. So I then had to walk several miles out of town on the A23 before getting a lift. The nearest to home that the driver was going was Dorking in Surrey. So when I got there I trudged several miles along the A 25 to Merrow outside Guildford. By this time it was late afternoon – and I was completely knackered. In the end I rang Dad who came down in the car to pick me up.

Another peril of hitching was that you never knew who was picking you up. On one occasion on my way back home from the sea I was given a lift by this avuncular looking oldish fellow. After a few minutes he started to stroke my thigh.!! I got him to drop me at the next set of lights. The only time in my life I have ever been propositioned by a member of my own sex. Yukk.!

Sunday Sunday —

Nothing ever happened on a Sunday back then. Sundays were the only days where the working population got to lie in bed. Not that there was a great deal – or indeed anything much at all – to do after they got up. The Lords Day Observance Society and the Bishops in the House of Lords saw to that. (*Yes, them again!*) The Bible laid down that Sunday was a day of rest. All shops were shut. No Sport was allowed. Cinemas, Theatres and other places of entertainment remained closed. In many areas even the Pubs did not open. You got up, had breakfast, went to Church, then returned home while Mum cooked the Roast with all the trimmings.

The only allegedly bright spot of the day came before lunch, with the "Billy Cotton Band Show" and its eponymous presenter and his famous cry of "Wakey Wakey" on the radio. After lunch you either went for a walk, did a spot of gardening, listened to the Forces Overseas requests programme on the Light Programme as it was then, mooched about, had tea, read a book and went back to bed. The main highlight of the evening was "Family Favourites" on the Radio presented by Charlie Chester. I keep telling you all, the pace of life was completely different in those days.

*

Our other major weekend relaxation was of course going to other people's parties. Between us we could rustle up perhaps 25 – 30 contacts, situated from the fringes of South London to midway to Sevenoaks. They provided us with an all encompassing intelligence network that provided detailed background on which private social events were taking place that Saturday night. If there was a party within a 10 mile radius we would hear of it. Address, often with the name of the person giving party, would adults be present. For almost four years this network delivered on a regular basis. As far as I recall, we only ever got shown the door a handful of times. Nor did we actually ever get INVITED to one. Normally when we turned up with a few bottles or a 4 pint "Pipkin" of beer they let us in.

We partied in Orpington, Petts Wood, Chislehurst, Bromley, Bickley, Elmstead Woods, Farnborough, West Wickham, Croydon, Keston, Eltham, Blackfen —— and these are just the ones I remember (there were quite a few locations which I couldn't even remember the following morning) We were the vanguard of the 60s. Cheers!!

Most of the parties we gatecrashed passed peaceably – the phrase "fighting drunk" never seemed to apply. Spewing drunk, paralytic drunk, maudlin drunk - all of these were commonplace. There simply was not the aggression in society generally that there is today. There was one guy who occasionally knocked around with us whose name if I remember correctly was Ian Sinclair. He was a complete dipsomaniac. We always had to carry him out of parties – sometimes we just thought sod it and left him on the pavement. Then one day he just disappeared from the scene – never saw him again. Perhaps he had signed the pledge?

Girls were clearly one of the main reasons for partying. There were a few girls who knocked around with us – Patty B, Sandy, Carole were perhaps the most memorable for their affectionate natures!

Not to forget Sally – aah yes. But there were plenty of others we met along the way. In those days girls dressed like girls – frocks with layers of petticoats, blouses that could easily be unbuttoned. Innocent – and not so innocent - memories still come flooding back.

Sandy was not a very bright girl. I recall that we were once driving down the High Street in JV's car with her and Carole in the back. As we drove along, one of the old Packards from the Hire Business pulled out in front of us. "Look" said John "there's one of those Hire Cars" Sandy looked over my shoulder, then said "Ooh yes, it is a bit tall isn't it"! John nearly crashed the car!

Another time we were walking back from another boozy evening. On the way we had met Sandy who had been out late with some other guy who had parted company with her. Not very chivalrous. She took my arm and we walked on as a group. As we got to her house her Father came rushing down the drive and started to accuse me of seducing his daughter and getting her drunk! There was no calming him down – I beat a swift retreat. When I think of how many Fathers I COULD have crossed swords with mind —

There was one *soirée* I do recall though with which none of us would want to be associated. I was sitting on a chair arm in the lounge chatting up a girl when all of a sudden a dressing table flew past the window and embedded itself in the lawn. A wardrobe followed and then a double bed. In anticipation of the neighbours phoning the cops, we beat a swift retreat.

Another evening provided some amusement – except maybe for the people involved. One of my closest mates named in this book – *he knows who he is* - had got between the sheets with a girl we had met at the party. This had rather annoyed the guy who was already in there with her.! A rather heated dispute as to squatters rights then occurred across the body of the poor girl who lay there between the two of them! She resolved the dispute by getting out from under and fleeing into the loo in her underwear. By this time the sound of arguing had caused a small crowd of us to gather in the bedroom doorway. Much mirth ensued. No blows were exchanged.

Meanwhile Johnny Sachs had found himself a new girl friend in the Eltham area. Sharon was a great looker – and had some very sexy friends. As far as I recall only he and I went to her house. There was one girl who had the nickname "Bubbles". I have absolutely no intention of telling you why.

The course of true love did not always run smooth for everyone of course. Breaking up is always hard to do as the song goes. Maybe the clearest example of this at the time was that of Tim Page. He was a year younger than me, and I never really knew the guy except in passing – he lived near Brian Calver in Green Street Green. It was he who told me that Tim had been going out with the same girl since childhood. He was completely smitten. Then she dumped him – in late 1961 if I remember. Tim was completely distraught, and the following year, at the tender age of 18, he left the UK for good. He finally ended up in Cambodia, where he worked for a while as a photographer for a local magazine.

Tim Page went on to become one of the most internationally acclaimed War Photographers in Vietnam. US sources said that he took insane risks on the field of battle. Anyhow, by the time he turned 21 he had been seriously wounded in action four times, and spent a year in the US having neurosurgery before becoming (perhaps unsurprisingly after what he had witnessed and endured) a member of the Anti War Protest Movement in the country. I believe he is still with us and now lives in Oz. Heartbreak can be a terrible thing.

In September 1960 I began my last year at Chis and Sid. I was already beginning to wonder whether I really wanted to spend the next three years studying ever more obscure literary tracts of three European nations. (The French literary device of *"cadence majeure"* and *"cadence mineure"* that we studied at S Level maybe had a lot to do with that view). When all was said and done, it was the beginning of the Swinging Sixties. After a decade of enforced self denial did I really want to spend another three years of self imposed academic monasticism? Or did I want to have a good time and pay my own way?

(I of course kept this to myself – Pedley would have had me crucified at the next Assembly for heresy had he known my thoughts.)

So I soldiered on with the course work and there were mock A levels in January. I already knew that I had a talent for languages that the school had nurtured. For which I am today truly grateful. The grounding has proved indispensable. Over the coming decades I would live and work in Frankfurt, Madrid, Paris, as well as in Geneva and Lucerne in Switzerland. Then go on to do business in Germany, including founding and running two companies there, for over 20 years.

There was a minor scandal at the start of the new School Year when Nig Pollard returned from a summer job working at Botton's Fairground in Great Yarmouth with a tattoo (shock horror, in 1960 only sailors and convicts had them). Pedley, being his usual sanctimonious self, made him remove it as a condition of coming back – poor old Nig had to have a skin graft. The irony was that he did not go on thereafter to complete the A level course.

*

In the World at large, on 12 October 1960, at a Plenary Meeting of the UN General Assembly in New York, the Soviet Premier Nikita Kruschev became incensed when the Philippines delegate delivered a speech condemning the USSR for having "enslaved" Eastern Europe. He took over the microphone on a point of order and delivered an angry rebuttal, including the words "X*ob tva maj*". Not surprisingly perhaps the simultaneous translator simply ignored the phrase and never put it into the record. You could see why. I will leave the first word to your imagination - the second and third words translate as "your Mother"

Kruschev was also alleged to have taken off his shoe and banged the table with it. This latter might be apocryphal.

1961

On January 1 1961 another eventful decade dawned for Planet Earth.

The year opened with John F Kennedy arriving in the White House.

Followed by the news that the US had launched the first Chimp into space so as to test the re-entry capsule for future space missions.

Also in January OPEC, the Organisation of Petroleum Exporting Countries originally formed in Iraq the autumn before, set up its offices in Vienna. The organisation that would go on to bring the economies of the Developed World to their knees in the 1970s was up and running.

In February the US tested the first Inter Continental Ballistic missile. The Space Race and the most dangerous chapter of the Cold War had begun. This was re-confirmed by the arrival of the first Polaris submarine at Holy Loch in Scotland.

On 9th February a seminal music event also took place – the Beatles made their debut at the Cavern Club in Liverpool.

In April the trial of Adolf Eichmann began in Jerusalem. His defence of "only obeying orders" was rightly rejected.

On 12th April the Russian cosmonaut Yuri Gagarin became the first man to circle the Earth in orbit.

While on the 17th April a rag tag army of Cuban exiles bank-rolled by the CIA invaded Cuba to retake the island from Castro. By 19th April it was all over – the Bay of Pigs operation as it had been named had turned into a total fiasco and a severe diplomatic disaster for the new President.

In June the star dancer of the Kirov Ballet Rudolf Nureyev defected and sought Political Asylum in Paris.

However, the three major events of 1961 that would have the most lasting impact on World affairs would come later in the year —

In August Britain applied to join the European Economic Community for the first time. This was vetoed by President de Gaulle. "Non!" was the headline of every newspaper at the time In the same month De Gaulle only narrowly avoided assassination in Paris by the OAS, the Organisation of the Secret Army who hated him for giving Algeria Independence.

A unique French invention saved his life. The OAS gunmen shot out the offside rear tyre of the armoured Citroen DS. But due to its *Hydrolastic* suspension holding it upright the car carried on on three wheels in a straight line. (*Now THERE'S a unique selling point for you!*)

On 30th August the East German Government began work on the erection of the Berlin Wall, which would in a few months completely isolate West Berlin from the rest of the world. The Soviets stated that the wall was being built "to keep out fascist elements conspiring to prevent the will of the people in building a Socialist state in East Germany"

The real reason for the wall had been somewhat different. It was built to keep the people IN, not to keep "Fascist elements" OUT. Up until then far too many East German citizens had been defecting from their "People's Democracy" to freedom in the West by crossing into the three Allied Zones of the divided City controlled by the US, Britain and France. The Wall would stand for 28 more years, and Berlin became Flash Point No 1 on the NATO list.

Finally, in December the first 400 US troops arrived in Saigon as "Advisors" This was the first action of what would become a full blown war in Vietnam that would last more than a decade, cost over 50,000 American lives, and end in humiliation for the US.

Thus did another eventful year pass. Not least in Hollywood. "West Side Story" took the Oscars by storm. Winning Best Picture. A more sombre film however provided the Best Actor. This went to the German actor Maximilian Schell for his role as the Defence Attorney for Nazi War Criminals in "Judgement at Nuremberg" Others not to forget were "101 Dalmatians" - which took four times as much at the Box Office as any other Movie that year - "Guns of Navarone" with Gregory Peck and Anthony Quinn, and "La Dolce Vita" with Anita Ekberg.

*

On 11th April I turned 18. I could now drink legally in a Pub. Having been banned from the Anchor and Hope that day by an over zealous barman, as previously related, a group of us ended up in the "Daylight Inn" in Petts Wood the following Saturday evening. The beer flowed freely – as ever. I do however still remember one or two things about that evening.

The first is that a couple of girls overheard one of us saying "let's find a party". "What sort of party?" one of them asked.

"Mixed" said Graham – in his usual sardonic fashion. The girls looked at each other, somewhat bemused, then the other said "What, Mods AND Rockers?" *(the comical nature of this statement will be appreciated by those over 60)* We all fell about laughing.

The second came later in the evening after a hard drinking game of Cardinal Puff. As I left the "Daylight" the freshness of the night air made me come over all funny as my old Granny used to say. Then I and several of my companions – none of whom I shall name to spare their blushes – stood in a circle outside the side door of the Pub and had a celebratory spew up

Another feature of pub life was cards. Three card brag and Pontoon were our games of choice. Most pubs would not let us play more than cribbage for the statutory pennies, so The White Hart in the High Street became our Casino of choice. We played for quite high stakes considering none of us had any source of income – up to Half a Crown a hand sometimes. This big nickel - silver coin was the mainstay of an evening out. In today's money it was worth just 12.5p. But that bought two pints of beer and a packet of crisps - with change - in 1961. In fact it bought more than that. The buying power of the currency in those days was greater than it is now. So to win a pot with a couple of those in it was a good evening's work. I, Graham, Harry, John Baker, his brother Bobby, Colin, Howard – we played for hours at a time.

A new face had joined the crowd – Nig Pollard. I think it is fair to say you could describe him as short but wiry. For a while he went out with Patty B – lucky chap. He had fair hair and just loved his cards. After one session I ended up owing him money. I would have paid him back the next time I saw him, but didn't know where he lived and did not bump into him for a while.

Imagine my amazement therefore when his big Sister knocked on our door one day and said she had come to collect his winnings! About 12/6d I think it was. She got the money. Pollard went down in my estimation that day – to send your *SISTER* to collect a debt?! He probably owed her the money.

(Nig Pollard emigrated to America a couple of years later. From what I understand his residence there later qualified him for the Military Draft for Vietnam. He decided this was not a good idea, so fled over the border to Canada. The last I heard of him he was living in the backwoods of British Columbia under a new name.)

Shillings and pence.

Talking of Nig Pollard's winnings, I feel at this point that I must explain to any readers under 45 the frankly byzantine system of money we had to work with until Britain went decimal in 1971. For them, and also for those readers in English speaking lands around the globe who never experienced the complexities of the "Old Money", here is a quick run down of our coinage in 1961.

Starting from the top and working our way down, there was the Crown. A Crown was worth Five Shillings. These coins were legal tender, but by 1960 no longer in general circulation. They were minted as Special Occasion coins from time to time. Still are today - eg Jubilee Crowns.

Then came the Half Crown. This was the highest value coin in general circulation and was worth Two Shillings and six pennies. This was what bought you a night down the Pub. Or a night at a B&B.

Next there was the Florin (named after a coin originally minted in Florence under the Di Medicis – why?) This was worth Two Shillings.

Then came the Shilling – known universally as a "Bob" as in "That'll cost you two bob Sir" - which was itself divided into Twelve (yes Twelve!) pennies. Just to confuse the issue further, there were Twenty shillings in One Pound – no coin, only available as a Banknote then. There was also a brown Ten Shilling note.

It did not end there. Next came the sixpence, known to everybody as "the Tanner". Like all of the above coins the tanner was called a silver coin. (They had been once but by the 1950s were nickel alloy.) Some silver sixpences did survive, and it was the custom to cook Christmas Puddings with a real silver sixpence inside them for some lucky diner to find. This survives to this day.

Then there was the strangest of all the coins of that era – the Threepenny bit. Worth three pennies. It was made from a brass alloy and had twelve sides. If you find one with a sprig of Thrift plant on the reverse it may be worth a "Bob or two" (*geddit?*)

Then there were the copper coins as they were known.

Penny coins – much larger than all the others (if you happen to come across one of the supposed three Edward VIII 1937 pennies still out there somewhere, Sothebys beckons). Halfpennies. And the humbler farthing, worth one quarter of a penny. The word comes from Anglo Saxon meaning a fourth part. Must have been worth something - back in 1066. The smallest coin, it had a Wren on the reverse. Farthings would in fact cease to be legal tender in 1961.

Could anyone ever have invented a more complicated or bizarre form of coinage than that? Twelve pennies to the Shilling, twenty shillings to the Pound? Long multiplication of money was a nightmare. How's your mental arithmetic? Using a pen and paper and the above info, multiply Twelve pounds

13 shillings and ninepence by 17, then divide 14 pounds five shillings and fourpence by five Then when you have stopped gibbering have a lie down.

Whereas decimal coinage has undoubtedly made our lives easier I cannot help but think that it has drastically lowered skills in numeracy generally. Calculators did not exist in the 50s or 60s. Our generation had to do sums like those above every day of our lives, and even sometimes in our heads. We all had well developed arithmetic skills – with the system of currency we had then we had no other choice!

(Footnote: whereas today shops price items with 99p on the end as in 5 pounds 99 to make them seem cheaper, shops in our day used to have "special offers" at 5 pounds 19 shillings and eleven pence. Somehow it doesn't seem such a bargain does it?)

Weights and measures

If that was not complicated enough, then try the Imperial system of Weights and Measures. This required yet more agility in mental arithmetic. Pay attention now –

Weight.

The basic measure of weight was the Pound. This was divided into 16 ounces. Or 14 ounces for gold and silver.

There were 14 pounds in a Stone.

There were 8 Stones in a hundredweight.

There were 20 hundred weights in a Ton.

Is there any rhyme, reason or logic in such a system?

None whatsoever.!

Length

Feet and yards were the two benchmarks. But it did not end there.

There were 22 yards in a chain

8 chains in a furlong

10 furlongs in a mile

Logic? – forget it!

A Furlong survives in horse racing to this day. How many punters could tell you what distance it represents is another story. A cricket pitch is 22 yards. A chain.

Liquid measure - this one is a doddle!

The basic unit has always been the pint. Divided into 4 gills.

A quart is 2 pints.

There are 8 pints to a gallon

So just to round off things nicely, please give me the price for 12 and a half yards of Dress Material priced at £3 14 shillings and sixpence a foot. Are you screaming yet?

Is it any wonder we were all so good at mental arithmetic in the 50s and 60s!?

Crunch time at school came in June 1961 when I sat my A levels. Once they were out of the way there was nothing left to do where school was concerned. All that was left was to await my results and then plan the rest of my life. I was mulling over whether or not to bother to turn up for the rest of the term, when suddenly fate intervened. One lunchtime I found myself in the dining hall,where my old nemesis dear old Milton was on dinner duty. He was stalking around on tip toe in his tracksuit being his usual pompous Welsh self. I cannot recall exactly what he said to me – probably berating me as usual for not having stood on my head for him even once in seven long and tedious gym years.

Anyhow, as an Upper Sixth former having just sat A levels I considered that I should have been due more respect. I must have thought enough was enough. All I do remember is that after a growing exasperation with the man I finally picked up a chair and threw it at him (sadly it missed) and stormed out of the school never to return – one of the more satisfactory moments of my life up until then I have to say.

This resulted in an extended summer break. So two weeks later I went to Great Yarmouth. It was not a holiday – but it would turn out to be one of life's defining experiences.

*

All the fun of the fair

The Pleasure Beach at Great Yarmouth was owned in those days by the Botton family, based in Green Street Green, a village just outside Orpington. Nig Pollard gave me an introduction to see them, and I was interviewed for a summer job by old man Botton himself. He was a tall, broad shouldered, imposing man, with jet black hair and saturnine looks that hinted at Romany blood He was clearly not a man to cross – as the knife scar down one side of his face confirmed. He took me on for the summer.

For those who are seeking to "disappear" for whatever reason, and either cannot afford the fare to Marseilles to join the French Foreign Legion, where they ask no questions, or maybe just do not wish to be shot at, the alternative has always been the fairground. I turned up in Great Yarmouth at the end of July with my sleeping bag and kitbag and was shown the trailer which I was sharing with a half dozen other guys. There were communal showers - two - and rudimentary toilet latrines. Butlins it wasn't.

Over the next few days I began to learn the tricks of the fairground. My main job was to collect the money on the rides – maybe the Management thought a nice middle class lad could be trusted not to rip them off. In reality the other guys would no more have ripped off Botton than jump off a cliff – in fact the latter might have been less painful. In any case they were too busy ripping off the punters.

It was known as tapping. In those days the rides were 6 pence or a shilling. (2.5p and 5p.) If the punter gave you a note (10 shillings or much less often One pound) then you gave him the change in one shilling or two shilling pieces. The punters were always eager to get on the rides, and were always in a good mood because of the surroundings they were in. So you counted their change into their hot sweaty palms – one coin at a time 1 2 3 etc.

The punters could feel the coins hitting each other and nearly always just shoved the change straight into their pockets. They never noticed that the last one or two had been tapped – the coin had been felt striking the others in the palm but had then been withdrawn again. The lads reckoned they could each make a couple of pounds a day this way – very good money in 1961. If anyone ever complained you just apologised for giving the wrong change. Easy!

It was as if the soubriquet "rough diamond" had been coined precisely for my trailer mates. One of them, Dave, did not appear to be as hard edged as the others. He would nervously look around him most of the time. I remember he told me that he was on the run for having sex with an under age girl – something that still got you a heavy sentence in those days. I also remember that he kept all his worldly goods in a tight wad of 10 shilling notes that he put under his pillow and slept on at night. Another "inmate" was big Irish Mick who worked on the roller coaster. I was later assigned to help him.

He had this girl friend in town and used to regale us all with tales of their clearly vigorous sex life. He used to keep complaining that she had been sleeping around behind his back because she was "woider down there than last time I saw her" It was a very useful adjunct to sex education with Doc King.

Like me, everyone in the trailer was a seasonal worker. In the Winter months only a skeleton crew stayed on to maintain – and protect - the rides. They were billeted in town. The Fairground had opened before I got there and would close again at the end of September. Most of the guys were out of the same mould. One step up from indigence as they earned a sparse living, they too carried their worldly possessions around with them. They were all young or youngish men, in their 20s and 30s. Many were illiterate, and as a "Grammar" boy I was often asked to read out letters and leaflets to them. Fairground life was hard, unforgiving work. 12 hour days were the norm. Sundays were free time. (Pleasure on a Sunday in 1961 was still banned by law.) I suspect that after their 30s most of my "colleagues" in Great Yarmouth ended up on the streets, in prison or in an early grave.

Every member of staff wore a whistle on a lanyard round their neck. Fairgrounds can be dangerous places to work on hot summer nights after the pubs closed. Fights with the Teddy boy gangs were not uncommon. They never lasted long. At the out-break of trouble a whistle blew and a dozen hard men armed with metal bars came running. I only had to use my whistle once – I was working on the Go Cart track when all of a sudden a couple of carts driven by very large men began to try and drive punters off the track. I remonstrated with them and they turned on me

Happily I had just been moving the straw crash bales with a large pitchfork, so I brandished this at them whilst blowing my whistle. They were thrown out of the Fairground – probably literally. There was no worry in 1961 about being arrested for assault when you were the aggrieved party, as is the case in our wonderfully PC era. (In fact in those days Police Constables themselves could clip wrongdoers round the ear and send them on their way - saving the taxpayer millions on paperwork.)

There was no 'Elf and Safety in those days either. Just as well, as it was on the Big Dipper that I earned my membership of the Fairground Workers Union. When I started to work with Irish Mick, we both rode the Big Dipper several times a day – sitting next to a pretty girl chatting her up and "consoling" her when she screamed with fright.

Then I began to push my luck a bit. To show off, I would stand on the ledge behind the last car, grip the rail tightly – and ride the coaster round the track. This drew admiring glances from my co-workers that clearly said "the boy is one of us".

My blood runs cold now just to think of it. It was over 70 feet from the ground at the top of the ride. The cars reached 45mph on the downwards tracks!

I worked at the Pleasure Beach for several weeks – it was a Master Class in how the other half lives. Although my co workers were itinerants, from the bottom rung of society they were not tramps or winos. Like all other strata of society there were the good guys, the sympathetic guys – and the real bad boys. Yet there were few disagreements between the crew. They worked long hours, watched each others backs (much as they would have done in the Foreign Legion in fact) They slaked their thirst in local Pubs, and often rolled back drunk to the trailer to add the smell of stale beer to that of stinking Farts and Weapons Grade BO. Yet any blood spilt almost always came from drunken punters.

There was however one guy, Reuben was his name, who apparently was related to old man Botton himself. Everyone gave him a wide berth and never dared to cross him. When I asked Irish Mick if this was because he was part of the Botton clan, he replied that was not the main reason. Apparently he had a history of taking a terrible revenge on anyone who thrashed him in a fight.

He would bide his time, then one night, as his victor was walking down some dark street, Reuben would be waiting round the next corner - with a brick in his hand. I did not know if that was true – but made a mental note never to upset him.! Fairground boys took no prisoners. With their lifestyle, I expect most of the guys I worked with that summer are long gone by now anyway.

*

As a final reference to Chis & Sid, in the summer of 1961 an interesting social survey was carried out for the *Chronicle*, the official school newspaper. It gave considerable insight into both the predominant Social Group of the boys at the school, as well as into the changing lifestyles in the average household at that time. The most common newspaper was the *Daily Telegraph*, read in 25% of the boys' households and by over 50% of the staff

Nearly every house now had a TV. This was having a profound effect on eating habits. There was a steady increase among "the square eyed" as they were known of eating on your lap in front of *Coronation Street*. The days of family meals around the table were coming to an end.

The A level results came through in August. I had always known that getting A Level in Spanish from scratch in 2 years would be a stretch. I guess that I had been less than inspired by the set books in German. I got an O level pass in each. French I had waltzed through at S level with flying colours. This would not be enough to get a University place – about which, although my parents were of course disappointed, I felt strangely relieved. The world was now my oyster.

The first job I had to raise some cash was on the night shift at Tip Top Bakeries on the local Industrial Estate. Several of my ex schoolmates, including Brian Calver, were on the line with me. We wore heavy duty gloves, yet I still bear the faint scars from burning myself on red hot tins coming off the conveyor belts in the ovens.

Then I found a job as a Ward Orderly at Farnborough Hospital – wheeling a corpse down to a darkened Mortuary in the middle of the night is not something you easily get used to. On the other hand the Nurses Home was a suitable compensation. The rest of the year passed without further incident. Work, evenings down the pub with the crowd, partying on Saturday nights. The simple life.

1962

Early in 1962 Dad helped me to get me a real job in the Export Invoicing Department at Glaxo Allenburys in London (Glaxo had recently acquired Burroughs Wellcome after swallowing Allen and Hanburys, to set them on the way to their present status as a "Big Pharma" leviathan.) Their offices were in Mayfair, at 47 Park Street W1. My language skills would be very useful here.

I of course had to commute from Orpington every morning. Up on the 7.48 to Waterloo East, then the "Drain" to Bank, followed by the Central Line to Marble Arch. 90 minutes each way. Crammed nose to nose on the Tube, where smoking was of course still permitted. (Yes I did as well) On the train up from home I could see that little had been done in almost 17 years since the war had ended to even clear some of the bomb sites the Luftwaffe had left behind, let alone redevelop them. London was still hurting.

Have you ever seen anyone using a Comptometer? Unless you are at least over 50 I very much doubt it. If you are under 40, then no way. In those pre-computer days it was a bulky but sophisticated numerical calculator with a banked keyboard. It could do every type of calculation that you can do on a pocket calculator – including "add to memory" with sub-totals. An experienced female operator could do them as quickly as you could on an early *Casio*. Quicker probably, because as far as I am aware there never was any calculator that could give results with Pounds shillings and pence. Anyhow it was brilliant to watch! Given that we were working in a multi currency, multi tax environment, with a whole array of discounts, she was the most important person in the office.

It was in this job that I first came to understand the true principle of Flexitime. The iron fast rule was that you had to be in the office by 9 AM at the latest. Once there however, when you started work was flexible. Everyone in the office except for me and my boss were women. They would arrive on time – then spend the next hour or so chatting about this and that and sipping endless cups of tea. Before typing away on their – manual – machines. They were there 8 hours a day – they actually did something constructive for maybe only 60% of the time.

When you leave your office today and you want to know the latest news you simply take out your I -Pad and click the 24 hr News Service of your choice. When I used to leave my office in Park Street Mayfair at 5 o'clock in the afternoon in 1962 there would still be almost 50 years to go before such technology was invented. So I would buy an Evening Newspaper from a vendor in the street who would constantly cry out "News, Star and Standard!" Three separate papers, each with three afternoon editions and a Late Night Final Edition at around 5.30. The three papers vied for readership – although somewhat oddly all of them seemed to rely on the independent street vendor. The only one to survive today is the Evening Standard – which is now a free give-away paper and a shadow of its former glory.

Stop Press - Orpington becomes the official centre of the World.

As everyone who lived there in the early 1960s knows, as well as all those regular viewers of "That Was the Week that Was" on a Saturday evening, Orpington became the official centre of the World in the spring of 1962. This was first conclusively stated to be so on BBC News Night one evening in March after the polls had closed in a local By Election. The result had been that Eric Lubbock, a Liberal, was elected as our MP. In 1962 a Liberal beating a Tory in what had always been a Tory safe seat was an earth shattering political event. This statement was then satirised by David Frost drawing an outline of the World with us at it's centre. on "That Was the Week that Was". Quite right too.

Eric Lubbock remains an unloved man in the Shires to this day. He was the main protagonist of legislation in 1968 to force local authorities to provide sites for Gypsy encampments. After his election victory he had been described as "Orpington Man", and journalists in the 60s went on to use the term as a disparaging way to describe the lower middle class. (Lower middle class? Us?!) Certainly nothing could have been further from the truth in his case. Son of the heir to a Barony, he became the 4th Baron Avebury in 1971.

Meanwhile the Swinging Sixties were getting up speed —

In January the first episode of Z Cars was screened.

In February the Sunday Times published the Nation's first colour supplement

In June the Beatles recorded at the Abbey Road Studios for the first time – and the first series of Steptoe and Sons was screened

In July the Rolling Stones made their very first public appearance – as a warm up act for Long John Baldry!

Also in July the first live transatlantic broadcast via the Telstar satellite occurred.

Last but far from least, Mary Quant, the fashion designer who would become an icon of the 60s by inventing the miniskirt and hot pants – earning the undying admiration of a whole generation of men in the process - opened the third branch of her "Bazaar" chain in Chelsea.

TV brings me back to Will Smith. He was someone I got to know better in the last year at school. He had been in Upper Sixth Science and had sat his A levels at the same time as me. We would stay in touch for several years afterwards. I remember that I rode pillion on his 500cc Triumph motorbike all the way from home down to St Ives in Cornwall, where we camped out for two nights over a long weekend.

I must confess though that Will had one other very important point in his favour. As time went by his family was one of the first in the area to have *Rediffusion* Cable TV installed. The forerunner of today's ITV channels. If I sometimes turned up at his house in Ramsden Road in the early evening at around the time Ena Sharples and Co were on – well it was simply coincidence!

En Route

For our summer holiday in 1962 Harry and I decided to hitch down to St Tropez. The second week in July Dad drove both of us of us down to Dover in the Ford, accompanied by Graham who was hitching down to Italy where I believe he was visiting relatives on his Mother's side. To say that the Channel crossing was rough would be an understatement. The crew was surprised they had sailed at all. Graham reminds me that I went a bright shade of green on board. We said goodbye to Graham at Calais, wishing him *"bon voyage"*

He also reminded me that under the unwritten rule of hitching one person is more likely to get a lift than two. So he set off

ahead of us up the road so as to give us first pop. It was therefore with a deep sense of pride in being British that we watched
him as he disappeared from view around the bend in the road,
clad in walking boots, shorts and T shirt, with a Union Jack
pinned to his rucksack: and a genuine colonial pith helmet
stuck on his head!.

(Graham eventually reached Rome, but declines to say just
how good a time he had there. Ah, *la dolce vita*)

By this time it was late afternoon. We had a sleeping bag roll
and a rucksack each, containing a flimsy one man tent, the
poles attached to the back, a portable cooking stove with spare
gas canisters, a few changes of clothes – that was about it. The
rest of the day was not very productive – by nightfall we had
only reached Beauvais, just over halfway to Paris. Just outside
the town we came upon a lay-by containing a large heap of
road gravel. Here we stopped to brew up and to munch on
baguettes we had bought along the way. By then it was dark,
and we could not see where to pitch a tent. We finally slept on
the gravel. This was not as crazy as it sounds – smooth road
gravel has a give to it so that you can wriggle your body shape
into it like a cheap mattress.

When we awoke the next morning early, we got a good opportunity to study at first hand the passing cars. The predominant
vehicle in France at that time was the Mk 1 Citroen 2CV. The
bodywork appeared to be cast from Corrugated Iron - which
clearly rusted quickly. It came in one colour – faded blue. It could
manage maybe 75 kph – eventually. As we witnessed for ourselves time and again throughout our trip across France, it was
the vehicle of choice for every French peasant – with the top
down you could get a bale of hay or a sheep across the back seat.

For those who could not afford a car, there was always "*le velo
Solex*". It was NOT a moped, but a standard bicycle, with a

tiny two stroke engine unit fitted over the front wheel. It could reach 25km per hour and had a fuel consumption of over 200mpg. Some girls even rode it side saddle like a horse! Over 8 million of these were sold. They remain perhaps the cheapest form of motorised transport ever built. So much so that when the owner died, the company was bought by the Japanese company Yamaha – who promptly closed it down.

There are still millions of peasants in France today, many of them scraping a living from a few hectares - and getting healthy subsidies from the EU under the Common Agricultural Policy. (CAP) You can blame Napoleon for this. The French law of inheritance is based on the *Code Napoleon*, which states that when a man dies his Estate must be divided equally between all of his children. So, when a Farmer leaves an estate of – say – 50 hectares and has three sons (which would not be unusual as France is still a Catholic country) each will get 16 and a bit hectares. Now fast forward two generations, and you can see why there are a million farms in France not much bigger than a market garden. All of these farmers - and their wives and families - have votes and form a militant group. Which is why France will not vote against the CAP until well after Hell freezes over.

We resumed hitching around 8.00 AM. Our first objective was the Gare du Nord in central Paris. Which we reached mid after-noon. From there we took the Metro to the Gare de Lyon, then a local train out to Fontainebleau where we over-nighted. The next morning we set out along the the Route Nationale 7 towards the Med. The N7 in 1962 was typical of French main roads at that time. Many have retained the same layout to this day. It was essentially a three lane road with staggered over taking in either direction.

This is perhaps THE most dangerous form of road layout ever devised by Traffic Engineers. It has been delivering a high death toll for decades. This gave the old Route N7 another, less welcoming soubriquet in the holiday season - "Route de la mort" or Road of death.

An additional danger on French roads at that time had been the deadly rule of *"Priorité à Droite"* that was still universally in force on all French roads in the 1960s. This rule of the road – which everyone accepts has killed far more Frenchmen than ever died at the Battle of Verdun in the First Great War – meant that any vehicle pulling out from a side turning into traffic had right of way. The idea had been that this would make drivers slow down when a side road was signposted.

It was a fatally bad idea. The principle of *Priorité à droite* became so engrained in drivers' minds that they often pulled out into traffic from side roads without even slowing down!! The rule was removed from almost all main roads in the early 70s, which now carry yellow diamonds on the road signs and signs marked "Passage protegée" - except at roundabouts. But the rule can still catch you out in the middle of towns where the rule is still enforced. As if the above was not bad enough every French driver drove like Jehu with a bee in their crotch. Road travel really was a life and death affair in France in the 60s. Still is.

One of the plus sides to driving across central France in those days however was that long stretches of road were lined on both sides with mile after mile of tall slim poplar trees. These gave considerable shade to drivers in the heat of summer, as well as being very scenic. Nature's air conditioning. It was under the shade of such trees by the roadside in Fontainebleau that we met two German girls also hitching south. One of them was named Ingrid Schmidt as I recall. She took a shine to Harry and he gave her his phone number. Then in minutes they were gone, in the back of a car driven by a Frenchman doubtless fervent in his belief in cordial relations with the old enemy!

Believe it or not, but our first lift of Day 3 was to be in a blue
Rover 90 saloon with French plates. He took us to Montargis.
Then a green Peugeot 404 took us a lot further, to beyond.
Moulins. It was late afternoon so we decided to spend the night
where were were. The driver of the Peugeot said he was continuing South in the morning and would pick us up where he dropped
us at 9 the next day. We camped overnight, feasting on the French
staples of freshly baked baguettes and slices of ham from a local
shop. From another we bought fruit – peaches, apples and plums
at rock bottom prices. With so many peasant farmers food is still
as cheap and plentiful in France as it was then.

We waited the next day to resume the offered lift – he never
turned up of course.

We eventually reached the outskirts of Lyon on the evening of
the fourth day. We ended up having to pitch our tent in a field
in pitch darkness – and awoke to the gentle lowing of cattle.
Just cows fortunately. Later that morning a yellow Renault
Sports convertible stopped for us. The driver and his mate were
both Brits. We then enjoyed a nail-biting, switch back ride
perched on the back along the hairpin bends of the section of
the N7 that runs through the foothills of the Massif Central to
Vienne, then down the Rhone Valley to Montelimar, the home
of Nougat. Here they dropped us off. It was only then we
noticed that he was driving in bare feet.

It was later that day outside Montelimar, at Pierrelatte, that we
perhaps got our most interesting lift. As we were walking up a
steep incline on the N7 just outside the town, a heavy lorry
with a giant trailer crawled alongside us. I began to chat to
the driver, asking him where he was going and could he give us
a lift. He was going all the way to Marseilles. After a bit I stood
on the protruding step by the driver's door and began to plead
our case more plaintively. In the end he relented and we both
jumped aboard just before the rig started to speed up again.

It turned out that he had been delivering pipes to the first Nuclear Power Station in France, being constructed at Pierrelatte itself, and was now returning to his depot in Marseilles. The 170km trip took over 4 hours in the brute of a lorry, by-passing Avignon to Aix en Provence, later turning off the N7 and finally to Marseilles. We then wended our way to the other side of the city to his depot. There were no articulated lorries on the roads in 1962, and he blocked all traffic in the surrounding streets for 20 minutes as he tried to reverse the rig. At one point he got into a slanging match with a Gendarme who had arrived to investigate the cause of the traffic chaos. This was amusing for Harry and I to watch – the waving of arms, the gestures, the air thick with *argôt* as the driver indulged in the time honoured tradition of "*s'enfoutisme*" characterised by much shrugging of shoulders, raised palms outstretched, interspersing speech with the occasional "*bof*". Eventually he got the trailer through the gates and the Gendarme left.

At the end of Day 5 we had finally reached the Mediterranean. Around 700 miles from Calais across the length of France. I recall that we actually ate a hot meal in a small bistro that night to celebrate before finding an official camp site. Tomorrow we would reach our final destination - almost.

The next morning we got the best ride any hitch hiker could hope for – in an empty air-conditioned luxury coach on its way along the Riviera highway to Cannes. What unadulterated bliss that was – the first time we had been cool in 5 days. We stretched out in the padded reclining seats and enjoyed the view. After about 100 kms we began to notice gigantic chunks of concrete, some as big as an office block, scattered randomly across the countryside. We were approaching Fréjus.

Almost 3 years earlier, in December 1959 a reservoir dam above Fréjus had collapsed, flooding the surrounding countryside and drowning over 400 people. The concrete débris we saw around us was the remains of the structure. (In fact much of that debris is still there today. Too large to move economically.) The driver dropped us off just outside Fréjus and continued his journey, our heartfelt thanks ringing in his ears. An hour or so later we arrived at *"Le Champs du Camping Saint Maxime"*, our home for the next week.

If you Google "St Maxime Camping" today you get several options, including two with swimming pools and all with shops and modern Toilet blocks. Like this in 1962 it was not. I remember a large open field on the edge of the town, fenced off with wire, the ground dry and the grass withered, with no facilities at all. Maybe there were toilets – but then open air French toilets in 1962 in summer would for us only have been an option of VERY last resort.

What I clearly do remember is that we had to sneak into a local Café on the Promenade on a daily basis to use their facilities – quick wash and brush up, clean your teeth then out. This was our only access to hot water. After the first couple of days Madame, the large Frenchwoman who ran the place, cottoned on to this and would rush towards the Wash Room door every time one of us was spotted entering the premises.

A guerilla war then ensued between her and us. In the end we had to buy coffees before we could gain entry. She may have been a good Catholic, but free hot water for the poor – *ie* us - *mon Dieu! C'est pas juste!*

Ste Maxime sits on one side of a small inlet in the blue waters of the Med, opposite *St Tropez* across the bay. St Trop as it was universally known had gained international celebrity in the late 50s and early 60s due largely to its most famous resident – the French sex kitten herself Brigitte Bardot. Her latest film "And God created Woman" had taken the world by storm. We did make a trip there the first day of our stay – but it was heaving with the glitterati of the early 60s, and my God, the prices in the shops and Bars!. We decided we would go on slumming it across the water.

We spent the next couple of days lazing around, soaking up the hot sun and recovering from our epic journey. We were still surviving on fruit, on fresh warm baguettes, filled with ham or cheese- and now as well on glorious fat, red *provençal* tomatoes. You bit into them and the juice ran down your chin. It may have been a peasant diet – but those peasants sure knew a thing or two. We bought a bottle of cheap red plonk and sat on the sea wall in the cooler evening air quaffing it.

There was one other food delicacy, available from a stall on the sea front, that I remember fondly - olive rolls. They stoned the olives, split them down the middle, then put them in a brioche type bun. The bun soaked up the olive oil. To this day I have never ever eaten anything more delicious. I am sure the surroundings had a lot to do with it. We could not have eaten more healthily if we had tried.

Swimming took up our more active moments. Like in many Med resorts, there was a diving platform moored a couple of hundred metres out to sea. I do not remember, but Harry tells me that we would race out to it – and that I often won. Me? Triumph at a sporting event? If only old Milton could have seen it!

On around the third or fourth morning Harry awoke and put his head out of the tent. As he stood up one of the largest hornets I have ever seen started buzzing around him. Harry was never one to put discretion before valour, and proceeded to try to catch it in a matchbox. Wrong!. The angry insect turned on him. Off went Harry, naked except for his boxer shorts, doing several circuits of the camp site while waving his arms furiously to ward off the creature. It is the one memory of Harry that will stay with me if and when all others have faded. Bloody hilarious! Harry eventually returned unscathed to the tent to find me doubled up with laughter. He was not amused.

I myself had adopted what I had been told was an effective deterrent for insects. *Gaulloises.* The black tobacco gives off an odour that is very unpleasant for mosquitoes – and marginally less unpleasant for humankind.

En retour

In 1962 ATM "Hole in the wall" machines were yet to be invented. Credit cards did not exist. It was the Golden Age of the Travellers Cheque. So when you were camping 700 miles from home and your cash was running low it could be a big problem. Which meant that after 8 days in *Ste Maxime*, and with a heavy heart, we had to start for home again.

It was late July, and so the whole of Paris and most of northern France had already arrived at the Mediterranean sunspots. Which meant that there was very little traffic going North. We soldiered on but it took us a day to reach Valence, halfway to Lyons. After a discussion we decided that one could probably get a lift easier than two. We each took our own clothes and possessions, and set off individually. After about two hours trudging along with thumb extended, a Bedford Minibus with British plates pulled up. I gratefully got in, over the moon at the thought that I was good for Dover! I did not spot Harry along the road, so he must have already got a lift.

They were an amazing bunch to find touring Southern France in 1962. The driver was in his forties I guess. His day job was as a Bus Driver in Oldham. (I was intrigued – busmen' s holidays really did exist then) Two young guys a bit younger than me sat in the back, together with their Mother and their

Grandfather. All the two young men talked of all the time was their love for Manchester United. They had three footballs between them. The bus was piled high with tins of Heinz beans, packets of cornflakes and various brands of English tea. This was unreal – in the middle of the South of France I had walked straight into an episode of Coronation Street!

We made Paris in two days. During that time they had been more than hospitable, sharing their baked beans and tea. In return I had bought baguettes and croissants in one or two of the villages we passed through, and done the translating when they stopped for petrol or shopping. So in an attempt to repay them for their generosity, I insisted on taking them sightseeing,.

Starting at the *Place de l' Étoile* (as it still was in 1962) where the eight *Grandes Avenues* converge, then down the *Champs Elysées* past the *Arc de Triomphe* into *Place de la Concorde*, then a sharp right halfway along *Rue de Rivoli* and down the Left Bank of the Seine, across the *Pont de Notre Dame* onto *Île de la Cité* and the great Cathedral of *Notre Dame,* finally ending up near the famous Terrace of *Palais des Chaillots* from which you get the very best view of the Eiffel Tower. We found a parking space and walked to the spot.

The two young lads stood there rapt for a minute or two. Then the one turned to the other and uttered the immortal words – "Ee, it's not as big as t' Blackpool Tower is it?" After all the hospitality they had given me I felt it would have been extremely rude to question this statement of faith in Northern British Engineering.

But it was North of the City on the N1 towards Calais that the mood changed and became more sombre. At Amiens we took a detour off the N1. Granddad was headed for a small village in *Picardie, Domart-en-Ponthieu*. A quiet backwater today, in the Summer and Autumn of 1916 it found itself slap bang in the middle of the 1st Battle of the Somme. There were in total ONE MILLION casualties in that carnage. He had fought in the battle, aged 19, and during the course of leave from the trenches had made friends with a local family. Would I translate for him? In a tearful reunion outside a house in the village, two old men embraced. I felt very humble indeed. This was surely what the *Entente Cordiale* was all about.

The next day we arrived in Dover. Where I said goodbye and many thanks to my friends from the North The lift all the way from Valence had been a godsend. It had saved me more than a day's time based on the outward journey. Their hospitality in feeding me had also conserved cash that I might have been forced to spend on food with a longer journey. As it was I had just enough cash left almost to the penny to buy a train ticket to Orpington and home. Harry got back a day later. He had ran out of cash on the third day. He tells me invested his last French franc in a big juicy peach from a market stall, and drank from Public fountains between hitches.

There were around 14 French francs to the £ in 1962. These were the New Francs that had been introduced in 1960, worth 100 old Francs. Prices had not yet started to reflect this, and in many shops and restaurants - pretty universally in fact – all prices were still being given in old francs. (In any case most of the French currency notes circulating in 1962 were still in old francs.) Confusing for foreigners at first. The older French generation thought in old Francs for the rest of their lives. As I recall, the entire 17 days (including return ferry/ train ticket) had cost me just under £ 24. This equates to just over £400 today.

The following Monday I went back to my office job in Mayfair. Browner leaner and fitter than I had been before I left. I had bought postcards for family that had been posted, but also bought some for the ladies in the Office. It filled up even more of their time with the morning chatter.

*

Almost to the day that we returned from France in August 1962, Soviet Premier Nikita Kruschev had announced that the Soviet Union was going to erect ICBM sites in Cuba. Fired from there the USA would have had no warning of a nuclear strike. President Kennedy reacted by establishing a Naval blockade around the island and warning the Soviets that any of their ships approaching Cuba would be stopped and searched, and then sunk if they did not turn about.

There then began three months of dangerous nuclear brink-manship between the two Super Powers as the world came ever closer to Nuclear annihilation. I will always remember standing on the terrace of the National Gallery in Trafalgar Square at one point during the crisis, surveying the centre of London with Big Ben in the background and wondering whether any of us would live to see the next day. In the end the Soviets backed down and in November their ships were recalled. The world breathed a huge sigh of collective relief. The Cold War continued for another 27 years.

Harry and I had just completed our mammoth summer journey under our own steam when in early August 1962 he very nearly died. One evening he was riding his BSA 350 motorbike without a crash helmet to a party in Orpington when he crashed it into a lamppost. He was taken to Farnborough Hospital where he lay in a coma close to death for a few days. His Mother was told that he was not expected to live. With supreme irony, on the very same day his Mother had been given the sad news, who should ring for him but one Ingrid Schmidt, the German girl to whom he had given his phone number when we had been hitching to St Tropez. the month before. His Mother told her the sad news and she never rang again.

But, hallelulia – Harry did not die. As he began to recover, several of us – me, Howard, Graham, Johnny Baker and others in the Orpington crowd, singly or in twos and threes, would visit him on the Ward and play 3 card brag on his bed. Howard and Graham once took him, still half paralysed, out of the Hospital in a wheel chair and wheeled him down the road – in his dressing gown – to the nearest Pub to have a pint. Now THAT'S convalescence for you!

Harry is Scottish by blood. He was born in Abadan in what was then Persia where his Father had been a Senior Engineer for an Oil company. His Mother always seemed to me to be rather straight laced. I always felt there was a touch of the Kirk about her. His elder brother was also a little dour - and an Accountant. The only thing in his favour was that he drove a mint condition Lanchester 14 saloon. Harry was the antithesis of the rest of his family. He was a bit of a lad, who held his own - and like a true Scot his drink - with the rest of the crowd.

He had retained at least one trait from his Scottish blood – only Harry would ever ask in the midst of a game of brag if anybody had two halfpennies for a penny He also developed a pragmatic approach to picking up girls at parties. He would go round the room propositioning every girl in turn. Sometimes it worked.

Harry must be both the luckiest and the unluckiest man alive. If he had ever needed a motto for a shield it would have had to have been "Against all odds" Before the near fatal crash he had been replacing a toolbox on to a top shelf one day, only to turn round and see it fall on his back. Two vertebrae were displaced. Another time he — well I won't embarrass him further, you get the message. He suffers the consequences of that near fatal accident when he was 19 to this day. For years he had to wear callipers on his leg – so no more hitching Then he had ulcers on the leg that did not heal for a long long time. He now has to use a crutch to get about.

Yet within 2 years of his near fatal crash he was back on a motorbike – this time with helmet and sidecar. So if anyone had told me in 1962 that Harry would still be alive today, with two children and a sixth grandchild on its way in Canada as I write, I would have applied to have them committed. Jenny and I had dinner with him a few weeks ago now. To exchange notes on our hitch to France in 62.

In fact Jenny has known Harry exactly as long as she has known me – for he was with me the night we first met, in November 1966. A true testament to the human spirit is Harry. And a very lucky boy!

Meanwhile in Hollywood the British film "Lawrence of Arabia" starring Peter O'Toole and Omar Sharif scooped Best picture. Perhaps as a reaction to this blow to Hollywood, the Committee gave Best Actor not to O'Toole – whose very finest hour was in the eponymous role – but to Gregory Peck in the American film of Harper Lee's book "To kill a Mockingbird".

Other films of note in 1962 were the very first Bond Movie "Dr No" starring the incomparable Sean Connery as the "Secret Agent Licensed to Kill" James Bond 007. Also "Mutiny on the Bounty" with Marlon Brando as Fletcher Christian and Trevor Howard as Captain Bligh.

Last but not least there was Darryl F Zanuck's mighty pan-oramic War Film, "The Longest Day" a 3hr epic re-enactment of the D Day Landings of 1944. The film starred the cream of male actors from both the US and Britain as well as leading actors from Germany and France. (Who, uniquely for a Hollywood film, spoke throughout in their own languages with sub titles.) This is the greatest War film of all time.

All that jazz.

The 1960s saw a revival in Traditional Jazz. Whatever that is – it had evolved over a century from the blues, through ragtime and swing to the jazz music of the 60s. There were several jazz clubs we went to either collectively or on our own. They all had one thing in common – they were dens of iniquity. I can personally attest to that.

The wildest was at Chislehurst Caves. The caves are man made, and were excavated over a century or so to provide lime for the great building boom in London in the days of Queen Victoria and beyond. This is where you took / picked up girls. As you might imagine, there was limited illumination underground – just a line of lights leading you to and from the performance area. It was dangerous to stray too far into the tunnels on either side as they ran for miles. However at any point you could both slip 10 yards into the darkness and have total privacy — taking care not to trip over anyone already there. I remember one night with Carole —

The Bromley Court Hotel was the most upmarket – a contradiction in terms in the jazz world – but even here in a tightly packed but well lit auditorium there were still what we used to call "jazz groupies".

The Downe jazz club was upstairs in "The George and Dragon" pub. I suppose it was really more of a Folk club with occasional jazz performers. Downe's most famous son is Charles Darwin. He lived at Downe House for the last 40 years of his life, where he wrote *Origin of Species*. With that fact in mind he might have found the unlit Car Park behind the Pub an interesting case study in the subject after dark. I have particularly fond memories of Sandra, the girl from the service station down the road. She was in one respect at least the spitting image of Dolly Parton - or should that be two? Oh yes!

But the Granddaddy of all Jazz clubs was Ronnie Scotts in Soho It opened in Gerrard Street in 1959 and is still very much alive and kicking today (although sadly its eponymous founder died in 1996, and it moved to Frith Street round the corner in the mid Sixties.) Ronnie almost single handedly turned a defunct musical niche market into a mainstream musical success story. British artists like Johnny Dankworth, Humphrey Lyttleton and even Acker Bilk owed their popularity to Ronnie.

The Club took a year or two to really take off. In the early days the Musicians Union refused to permit US artists to appear in the UK. This was where the greatest Jazz performers had evolved. It took him several years to get this ban lifted - in return for the US Union allowing British artists into the States. From then on Ronnie Scotts became a must perform site for all the Jazz Greats of the period. I was privileged to go there just once – and stayed all night when the music just went on and on. One thing in particular that I remember of that visit was the cigarette smoke – as you sat there you could see the level of it sinking slowly against the floodlights, like water filling a tank upside down. Awesome. I completely forget who was playing.

1963

The Winter of 1962 – 63 proved to be the coldest since 1740. Temperatures slumped to -16c in places. The sea froze for a mile out from the shore at Herne Bay in Kent. The Thames froze from Kingston back to the source. The only thing that kept the Thames from freezing over were the warm water effluents from Battersea power station. From 29th December 1962 to 6th March 1963 temperatures never rose above freezing in some parts of the Country. We wore coats in the house for most of that time, as freezing to death was not an option. At one point we ran out of coal as the horse could not make deliveries. Imagine it – your only source of warmth taken away in the coldest part of the year. Like living in a deep freeze. But we survived. We British always do. The trains still ran. No "wrong kind of snow" in those days!

*

The New Year heralded another string of momentous global events. Segregation in the Southern States of the US took centre stage in January. George Wallace was elected as Governor of Alabama with the battle cry "Segregation now, segregation tomorrow, segregation forever" Then at the end of the month President Charles de Gaulle pronounced a firm "Non" to Britain joining the Common Market (*Had Gerard reported back on British food?*)

Beatlemania had taken off and the Liverpool lads recorded their first album "Please please me" - which would soon please their Bank Manager greatly. The most famous and indeed iconic of all railway engines in Britain "The Flying Scotsman" was taken out of service. Germany and France signed the Elysée Treaty that ended several centuries of conflict between the two countries.

In March 2003 six members of the OAS were sentenced to death in Paris for attempting to assassinate President de Gaulle. 5 were reprieved, but the ringleader was executed the military way – by firing squad. The infamous Alcatraz Prison in San Francisco Bay was finally closed. At the end of the month Dr Beeching – the man who would go on to decimate British Rail - first published his recommendations.

In April Winston Churchill was declared an honorary citizen of the United States, Yugoslavia became a Republic with Josip Broz Tito as its Life President. And Martin Luther King and some of his followers were arrested in Montgomery Alabama for parading without a permit – in other words for being black.

In May there was only one event of earth shattering importance – Bob Dylan released his second album "The Free Wheeling Bob Dylan"

In June Parliament and the Establishment were rocked to the core by the sudden resignation of John Profumo as Minister of Defence. Profumo had been a regular attendee at the notorious parties given by Steven Ward at Cliveden House in Berkshire, former home of the Astors. He had been having regular sex with a prostitute, Christine Keeler – who, it turned out, had at the same time been having sex with a senior Russian diplomat. The implication of this being that the resulting pillow talk could have seriously prejudiced the security of the Nation.

(This was at the height of the Cold War, with Britain on a 4 minute warning of a nuclear strike by the Communists.)

In August Martin Luther King gave his seminal address to 200,000 followers by the Washington Monument - "I have a dream"

On 8th August a gang robbed the Glasgow to London Mail Train and stole £2.5 million in used notes (worth around £40 million today.) This will forever be known as The Great Train Robbery. Three robbers were never caught, several were tried and convicted the following year and two subsequently escaped from prison. One, Ronny Biggs, fled to Brazil where he stayed for over 30 years.

President John Fitzgerald Kennedy was assassinated in Dallas Texas on 22 November 1963 – providing conspiracy theorists with unlimited material that is still running to this day. Some say the Mafia did it, others say the CIA did it. Some that Southerners did it because he supported de-segregation – the truth is nobody knows. Lee Harvey Oswald was arrested for having shot him from an upstairs window of the Texas Book Depository - only to be assassinated himself by Jack Ruby, a minor member of the Mob already dying from cancer, two days later. Yet more furthering the cause of the conspiracy theorists.

By my 20th birthday I was already getting tired of the daily commute. Out of house at 7.00AM, crushed up tight with my fellow man in packed carriages up to London Bridge, with everyone smoking like a chimney. Then crushed again in crowded Tube trains – still smoking - with a walk between lines through the long tunnels at Bank. Then repeated again at 5.30PM. The job was fine, but there was no real scope for using languages as I had hoped. Also, the hitch across France the previous summer had awoken within me a latent wanderlust.

The Oscar for Best picture was won in 1963 by the British film "Tom Jones" with Albert Finney and Susannah York. Best Actor was won by Sidney Poitier for "Lilies of the Field". Both these choices were rather unusual, and displayed a rare touch of aestheticism by the Committee. "Tom Jones" beat blockbusters such as "Cleopatra" with Elizabeth Taylor and Richard Burton in No 1 spot, "Its a mad mad World" (and a mad mad film, with Spencer Tracy playing the straight man,) in No 2, and "How the West was won" with Gregory Peck and James Stewart "in No 3.

"Lilies of the Field" did not even feature in the Top 15. It was the first time a coloured actor won the Oscar for Best Actor in a Leading role, and his second nomination.

In May I left Glaxo-Allenbury's - and joined Global Tours as a Travel Courier taking Coach parties around Europe. 5 countries in 12 days with 2 days turn round at home to do laundry. (*Maybe I will write a book about that summer one day.*) Suffice it to say that it did wonders for my language skills. By the end of September, on my last trip of the season to Lucerne in Switzerland, I clearly recall sitting at a table in the *Stadtskeller* Nightclub with several of my charges, our Belgian Coach Driver and local Swiss, speaking and translating simultaneously in French, German and English. Mission accomplished!

My earnings that summer were augmented considerably by tips, commissions on sales from organised shopping trips – and from selling excursions. So at the end of September I returned home with a fairly thick bundle of the large, navy blue coloured 100 Swiss Franc notes in my pocket. (At the time these 100 Franc notes were worth around £8 each. Today they are worth no less than **SIXTY NINE** pounds each – there's devaluation for you!!)

After a a couple of months mooching around I took a Christmas job in London. Then I met Her Majesty the Queen.

*

The Christmas job was in the Toy Department at Harrods. One afternoon all shop floor staff were asked to stay behind after the Store closed. We stood around kicking our heels for half an hour or so, then there was a sudden flurry of activity in the Department with the arrival of Senior Managers. Then our Monarch entered the Department

My first impression was how tiny she was. She was dressed all in black, as State Mourning for President Kennedy was still in force. She was only introduced to top Management, who escorted her around the exhibits. As I recall she ordered one of the top of the range pedal cars that had been converted to run with an electric motor. It would have accommodated up to maybe an 8 year old. It was rumoured to do 15mph. This must have been for Andrew, who was almost 4 at the time. Then she left. So I did not actually *meet* her.

After a quiet family Christmas I went to a party on December 27th. I remember that Westwood from my year at Chis and Sid was there. We had never got on, and we got into a – fairly civilised – argument about something or another. Then the party got a bit boring and I went back home.

While I had been out my Father had dropped dead from a heart attack at the age of 57.

1964

After we buried Dad in the Churchyard at All Saints, it was clear that I could not pursue my career in the Travel Business any further. Much as I had wanted to. Because of my language skills I had been offered a permanent job by Global in their Lucerne office. Mother was a widow at 50, and almost mad with grief. Phil was only just 16 and still at school. I was the eldest son. I needed to stay in Orpington. As I had had enough of the daily commute – I never returned to it ever again – I decided that something in Sales would give me more freedom of movement

Helping Mum turned out not to be so easy. She would not take comfort or advice from anyone and actually used to tell me not to meddle in "her"affairs. This was a bit hurtful really – not least because I had given up the chance to live and work in Switzerland to try to give her support. But as the poet said, love does not alter when it alteration finds.

Mum had always been strong willed – I think in no small part so as to be able to cope with Dad's very middle class family who had always considered her a bit *infra dig* (if you think the British Class system is bad enough now, you should have been around in the 1950s and 60s.) She could also be frustrating and mercurial at times. For instance, I had been suggesting to her for months on end that I and Phil should demolish the green-house at the bottom of the garden before it fell down. She would have none of it. One day I got back from work – to find that she had PAID someone to come in and do it. That was my Mother for you! Mind you, I guess I inherited my stubborn streak from Mum, bless her.

Mind you, she must have been scared stiff. Women of her era had never had to make any decisions re finance, bill paying or any other day to day activity outside domesticity. There was however one person to whom all widowed ladies of the time could turn – the family Solicitor. He – for there were no female lawyers at that time – was their rock. Mum trusted ours implicitly. He could do no wrong, and his advice was Holy Writ.

In April I became 21. The celebrations were rather muted in the circumstances. Shortly afterwards I secured a job with Coal Products, a division of the National Coal Board – and found myself driving a high sided 30 cwt van around Builders Merchants in the South East selling 10 gallon drums of *Synthaprufe*, then and now a critical building product for damp courses and roofing.

It was not a vehicle in which to pick up girls. However, as I had inherited Dad's Ford Popular this was not a problem. So as summer came round, I asked Mum if she could manage without me for a couple of weeks. By this time she had somewhat regained her equilibrium and got herself a little job at the hat shop in the High Street (now she was a widow it was no longer any social disgrace to work!) So I set off for Arcachon in the far South West of France with Joe Swain and Mick Haffner in tow. Harry, with Alan Smith beside him, followed on in his newly acquired Motorbike and side car. (This broke down near Rouen, and they had to abandon it there and hitch the rest of the way.) Pretty difficult for him with callipers on his leg The trip back home in the Ford proved a little cramped.

We took the Route Nationale 10 from Paris to Chartres, then on to Poitiers. On the way the road passes near Le Mans, and you drive along the fast stretch of the N 10 that is closed once a year to become the Mulsanne Straight in the 24 hr race.

In 1964 Arcachon was where the French went on holiday. They still do. The French call it *La Côte d' Argent*. On the Atlantic coast between Bordeaux and Biarritz, the Bay of Arcachon borders *Les Landes,* a long stretch of coast south of the town that has been planted with thousands of pine trees to anchor the sandy soil. This area is also famous for its sand dunes. The tallest is *La Dune du Pilât*, almost 450 feet high. Only we Brits would be mad enough to climb it in the searing heat. So naturally we did. We reached the summit gasping for breath and in a pool of sweat. I knew then just how much Lawrence of Arabia must have suffered!

It was so hot that summer. The camp site was like a furnace in the daytime. Pines give little shade. The car's 1960s plastic seats were too hot to even sit on. It was far too hot for lying around on beaches. The town had lots of narrow streets with the obligatory Brasseries and Bars. We would sit in the shade sipping beers and *mentes a l'eau* and ogling the girls.

We were all working by then, and so were not as poverty stricken as Harry and I had been two years before. As a result we mostly ate out in the evenings. At one place I ordered *aubergines provençales* as a side dish, thinking "ah, garlic aubergines, sounds nice". They must have pickled them in garlic for a month then fried them in garlic for a couple of days. They were positively eye watering. Knowing my French was good, Mick Haffner has ragged me about that dish ever since.

Then disaster struck. I lost the car keys. (*When my family read this they will all say - bloody hell, he was at it even then!*) In 1964 all cars on French roads were French built. If there had been a Ford dealer within 100kms they must have been keeping a very low profile. In the end a local garage came up with a temporary solution. Essentially they hot wired the engine and left the result in place. For the rest of the holiday anyone could simply have got in the car, touched the two wires together and driven away. To stop the engine I had to stall it by dropping the clutch.

To lock and unlock the car he provided us with a coat hanger – but I had to leave the back windows wide enough open to be able to hook the button on one door with it so I could get in. But in summer in France people left their car windows open all the time anyhow.

This arrangement served to get us back to the Channel Ports. Although the Ferry operator did not take too kindly to me either having to drop the clutch to turn the engine off or to having to hot wire it to start it up again. They took some persuading to let us travel.

*

Meanwhile the world at large continued to turn

In January the Great Train robbers (or the ones that had been caught) went on trial.

In February the British and French Governments agreed to build the Channel Tunnel – estimated construction time 5 years. It finally opened 30 years later.

In March the declining value of the British Pound was hinted at by the reintroduction of £10 notes for the first time since the War. There were pitched battles between Mods and Rockers on Clacton seafront. Prince Edward was born.

In April Liverpool won the Football League title for the sixth time (those were the days!)

In July the Beatles issued their latest album "Hard Days Night"

In August Peter Allen and Gwynne Evans were the last two prisoners ever to be executed in Britain. 6 weeks later and they would have escaped the rope. In October Parliament voted for a Moratorium on the Death Penalty.

Sadly the rest of us did not escape future punishment in October – Labour under Harold Wilson was elected into Government. The die was cast for many of the social ills that afflict us today. The Nanny State was born.

*

By this time, Orpington 127 never seemed to stop ringing My social circle was getting ever larger, Phil was developing his own – and then there were Mum's friends. Whenever one of them rang her she always answered the phone the same way. "Oh hello dear" she would say "I was just going to ring you". It used to crease me up.

When Jenny first started coming round to home, she had to control herself every time she heard it. "Oh hello dear, I haven't heard a word from you since 1937 - but I was about to ring you" she would mimic when we were alone in the front room. Between her friends Rene, Anne and Ross, Mum spent almost as much time on the phone as we did. And she ALWAYS answered the phone to her friends with the self same words. Religiously. Bless her.

There were an estimated 4 million phones in Britain in 1965. Outside of main Metropolitan areas most numbers were 4 digits maximum. Our line had been put in just after the War so we still had a 3 digit number. In those days local calls were dialled by the user but any long distance calls were made through an operator. You had to RESERVE overseas calls in advance. In many rural areas all calls went through an operator. (*I have today received a phone bill from BT with an item included in it for £23.71 for just FIVE calls to Directory Enquiries. In 1964 these calls were free – and were NEVER answered by Ranjit from Mumbai) Progress is relative.*

In London as recently as 1968 every exchange had its own name. British Telecommunications - then a part of the General Post Office – took the first three digits of the dialling code, and then using the alphabetic equivalents printed on the dial of your phone assigned it a name. There were Frobisher and Ivanhoe, Mogador and Monarch — and lots lots more I cannot remember.

The only other way you could make a call was from one of those now famous and iconic red phone boxes. They took old One Penny pieces, big clunky coins. There were two buttons on the side marked A and B. You put in four pennies for your call and dialled the number. When they answered you pressed Button A and got connected. If there was no reply, then you pressed Button B and got your money back. On a long distance call from a box you had to reverse the charges – otherwise you got about 30 seconds.

I keep telling you – it was a totally different World then.

Oscars

Hollywood kept the cameras rolling in 1964. "My Fair Lady" won the Best picture and Rex Harrison won Best Actor for his role in the film. There were TWO Bond movies released that year, first "Goldfinger" then "From Russia with Love". There was the seminal "Hard Day's Night" the first film made by the Beatles (personally I think they should have stuck to singing). Last but not least there was "Night of the Iguana" with Ava Gardner delivering the performance of her life and Richard Burton "welshing it up" as always.

Brothers

It occurs to me that I have only up until now referred to brother Phil almost in passing. In truth, the four and a half year gap between our births had a major impact on fraternal relations. Phil and I sat down after Mum died and we calculated that we had only ever spent 10 months in total together at the same school. He went to St Nicholas as I had done, and because he was born in November '47 did not get to Chislehurst Road Primary until September 1953. I remember walking him home from school at the age of 6 for that 10 months – then I took the 11+ and disappeared to Chis and Sid. Our paths scholastically never crossed again.

He failed his 11+ and in 1959 went to Cray Valley Technical School, located in the old C&S Building at Crittalls Corner. By then I was taking O levels and knocking around with a whole new set of mates: like most 16 year olds. We were chalk and cheese. I was more academically minded, more mercurial and a bit of a romantic. He was more practical with his feet on the ground. We never saw much of each other after that - even though we lived in the same house. Family holidays and Christmas were about it.

We never had too much in common to be fair – different educational backgrounds I suppose amongst other things. Yes there had been sibling rivalry – a lot of it generated by me sad to say. I remember one particularly ignoble occasion when Phil must have been around 5 or 6. We had put the tent up in the back garden. I started banging on the side of it with the handle of a rake, knowing full well he was inside at the time. I split his head open - and was not allowed out to play again for two weeks.

But the biggest source of tension between us perhaps over the past 30 years has been Mum. As I said before, our Mother was a very strong willed woman who always wanted her own way.

Phil always gave it to her. He waited on her every need - and I saw straight through her. He worshipped the ground she walked on, quite literally, whereas I would not always agree with her (*shock horror, send for the hangman!*). He never seemed to realise that you can love someone but not have to always slavishly agree with them. He remained oblivious to the fact that as a loving son I had given up job opportunities to support her after Dad died. Perhaps he had never realised I had done that?

This idiocy rumbled on for too many years. It was only when Mum started to become senile in her last years that we got together again in a common cause. Now we lunch occasionally and exchange holiday snaps. We are never going to be close – but then real life is seldom like an episode of the Waltons. We haven't spoken for quite a while.

*

By the mid 60s almost every town had regular Disco nights. Ours were held in the Civic Hall up behind the Railway station. (Conveniently located within 200 yards of the Maxwell.!) They always attracted big audiences. There would usually be a Star attraction. The one I remember most was Craig Douglas "the Singing Milkman".

Born Terence Perkins in 1941 on the Isle of Wight, his version of "Only Sixteen" released in 1959 reached Number 1 in the charts. It even outsold the original by Sam Cooke. Then in 1961 he entered the "A Song for Europe" contest with his own song. It came last. In 1962 he actually topped the Bill at the Beatles first major concert. But by the winter of 1964 his career was on the wane. (*Elvis never appeared at the Civic Hall Orpington*)

He went down well enough on the night. Until suddenly the audience formed a very large circle around two guys squaring up to each other. One was a notorious local thug from the Council Estate, who was always throwing his weight around in a Neanderthal manner: the other was the son of an influential shopkeeper in the area. He had the longer reach, and it turned out to be a draw after much huffing and puffing and many shouts of encouragement from those who would have loved to see their pet hate with his face smashed in.

The Russell girls lived nearby and were usually at Disco nights. Jane was a stunning blonde with a touch of the ice maiden about her, and much lusted after by all of us. Her sister Jackie must have taken after her Father – she was on the plump side and a bit plain. This did not matter to any of us. Getting off with Jackie was fine in itself – it also offered the future possibility of dating her sister. The Dating game could be quite cynical. Oh yes!

EPILOGUE

Which brings me to the end of this book, of this voyage through the past. Which as everyone knows is "Another Country." There can be no doubt that the immediate post war years and into the early 1960s were a more straightforward, more innocent era.

A time when Society in Britain had a seemingly immutable Order and Certainty about it. When all classes of society were united in the principle of God King and Country

A time when Crime was at the lowest levels ever recorded.

A time when almost nobody had very much and conspicuous consumption was practically unknown.

A time when a Half Crown could give you a night out at the Pub - or at a B&B.

A time when your local shopkeeper knew you by name, knew what you usually bought and had time to chat.

A time when 5 year old children could walk to school in safety, and the streets were often silent save for the clip clop of horses hooves or the occasional sound of a combustion engine or motor horn.

A time when the Church of England was still a powerful force in the land. And therefore a time when Christian values held sway in Society – when divorce was frowned upon, pornography had been excommunicated from the population, and abortion and homosexuality were still abominations and criminal offences.

It was a time when Shame still held a stranglehold over most social behaviour *(O tempora, o mores!)*

A time when most people were far more aware and solicitous of their Social Responsibilities than they were of their Human Rights.

A time when the punishment fitted the crime and murderers were sent to the gallows.

A time when Political Correctness and ' Elf and Safety had never even been conceived.

A time when the pleasures of the Open Road were exactly that

A time when Excellence was not a dirty word in Education.

A time when the Monarchy ruled over the Globe.

A time when the British Pound was still the strongest Global currency

A time when Family Doctors made house calls 24/7

A time when there was no paperwork involved BEFORE dealing with an Emergency.

A time when Teachers in schools were allowed to exercise authority, and children learned discipline. —

*

But it was also a time when British Society was institutionally racist.

A time when the majority of married women had no chance of a job let alone a career.

A time when there was still considerable hardship within the ranks of the Working poor (*which made the children who came from that background that qualified for Grammar School in 1954 all the more laudable*)

A time when what class you were born into determined how far you went in life - **the only credible way out of this impasse being the Grammar School system!**

It was also the time during which Britain squandered $ 2.7 Billion of Marshall Aid on delusions of Imperial Grandeur, and as a result ended up losing the lot – as well as the fiefdom over the greatest Empire the World has ever known.

Those years, and the following 5 decades, have moulded the Society that we live in today, and in which our children and grandchildren will have to live tomorrow. A present day Society that has made quite staggering advances since the end of the 1950s in Technology, Medicine, Aviation, Space Exploration and just about every other field of human endeavour.

But are we as happy and contented as my generation was? Looking around me it does not seem so. As the old Chinese proverb goes "Take what you will – and pay for it" Compared to the world of my formative years life today is undoubtedly much more stressful, and often plagued by uncertainty and anxieties. Time is always at a premium today, and the pace of life moves ever more quickly. There is no time for quiet contemplation outside of a monastery! Over 30 million vehicles clog our roads and pollute our cities. In the modern two parent family – married or otherwise – both parents have to go out to work to keep the wolf from the door. This has resulted in many more latch key kids and in pre school nurseries. Children are now viewed simply as consumer units by commercial companies, and are bombarded with in your face ads 24/7.

Maybe in time some of the virtues and qualities of life in the 1950s will creep slowly back into the public consciousness. I do hope so. For as I view the world today, we were the fortunate ones. We certainly had more fun.